TO JACK & JACKIE

WE, ON 'WALKING BREAKS',
WITH MONOLOGUES, OFTEN ONES MENTIONED 'WI
ENTERTAINER STANLEY HOLLOWAY IS DISCUSSED.
A VERY ABLE PERFORMER, THIS LITTLE BOOK
THERE IS A LOCAL CONNECTION, IN THAT S̄   , ᴧ QUEENIE WERE MARRIED
IN ST JAMES CHURCH CLACTON IN 1913.   NOT A LOT OF PEOPLE KNOW THAT!

AN ARM OF IRON

The life and times of the entertainer

Stanley Holloway O.B.E.

1-10-1890 to 30-1-1982

by

Roy Walding

AN ARM OF IRON

Published by T.H.E.,

Theatrical Heritage Entertains

October, 1996

Great Yarmouth

Norfolk NR 31 8 H*R*

For

Stanley, Sally, Adrian, Simon,

Harry and Eileen.

ISBN 0 9529166 0 6

Cover by Ivan Rodwell

CONTENTS

PREFACE

Something familiar, something peculiar, something for everyone, a comedy tonight

These words come from a popular song in the 1964 Stephen Sondheim show -

A funny thing happened to me on the way to the forum.

"Comedy Tonight" was one of the songs in Stanley Holloway's repertoire.

On a recent compact disc, he sings, in his rich baritone voice:-

"I have but one heart to give, but that heart is true,

I have who have one life to live, give that life to you,

Though no fabled wealth have I, share the world with me,

We can live most anywhere - I will have my own adventure."

The poignant words here, come from a 1934 musical - *The Three Sisters.*

This show in which Stanley appeared was by Jerome Kern and Oscar Hammerstein.

The sentiments Stanley expressed in songs written 30 years apart, seem to sum up

his attitude as an entertainer.

Stanley Holloway is probably associated by most people who know of him, with the

popular film - *'My Fair Lady'.* He made this when he was 74 years old, after

being in the record breaking stage show. The film version is often repeated on

television and is available on video.

Stanley nearly withdrew from his *chance of a lifetime* character part - Alfred

Doolittle - which brought him worldwide fame. Some older people do fondly

remember his amusing recitations about -

'Sam and his musket', 'Albert and a Lion' or some 'Brahn Boots'

Stanley Holloway spent sixty years working in all kinds of entertainment

His talented career shines like the facets of a diamond, in our British Theatrical Heritage.

Stanley Holloway travelled widely and has received international acclaim.

In this book I have shown how an ordinary cockney performer rose to such heights.

ACKNOWLEDGEMENTS

No book was intended until six months ago. Over the previous seven years I have collected snippets from all sorts of sources that it was not then necessary to record. I couldn't possibly find or trace them all for it would take many more months and pages.

I warmly thank anyone named in the book, or others who think they should have been given credit for helping piece together, as thoroughly and accurately as possible, the life of Stanley Holloway. The day the book is printed, further information will probably appear like lost pieces of a jigsaw. If it is a successful project, you will anonymously share in thanks from the Actors Charity, Voice of Progress for the blind and Asthma Research in which Stanley was interested and to whom contributions will be given.

Stanley Holloway's own book by Dick Richards was very helpful.

Sir Michael Marshall's books of monologues too were useful for reference.

I should like to thank the British Broadcasting Corporation Archives and Radio Times. Some oddments of articles passed to me may have come from old T.V. Times, theatre magazines, programmes, newspapers, biographies of other artists, critics etc etc.

Thank you too John Balls, Norwich and Norfolk authority on Gilbert and Sullivan and the Titanic disaster, for reading the first draft copy and offering advice.

Thanks to my wife, the book has been has read and re-read by her several times. As an impartial observer, knowing little of the subject material, Sally has helped so much.

Above all, I am extremely grateful to Harry Gresty for all his time, trouble and for sharing the many helpful references he too has unearthed from libraries over the last few years.

CHAPTER ONE

From choirboy to concert party.

On the 1st October,1890, Florence Holloway presented her husband George, a respectable lawyer's clerk, with a son. Their home was at 30, Wentworth Road, Manor Park, London East 12. The baby was named Stanley Augustus, after the famous New York Herald newspaper correspondent and explorer, Sir Henry Morton Stanley. He had found doctor Livingstone in Africa only twenty years previously. Young Stanley's christening service was held at All Saints Church, just around the corner in the busier Romford Road. This Victorian red brick building faced Woodgrange cemetery, one of the greener places in London. Young Stanley grew up in a *white collar* worker's house, not lacking home comforts. Steam trains took commuters like George Holloway from nearby Manor Park station to work in the grimy city. When Stanley was only three years old, he survived an unwelcome tumble into the sea off the pier at Walton-on-the-Naze in Essex.

Stanley went to Sunday school at the church and when old enough, joined the choir. Much later he joked - "I was put in the middle as a *surplice* chorister!" On the wall of the nave now, there is a framed photograph of Stanley in Eton collar, sent in 1982 by his wife Laney at the request of the vicar and churchwardens. It commemorates their choirboy who became an internationally famous actor and singer.

In 1900, as news came to the Holloway home of the Boer War happenings at Ladysmith and Mafeking in South Africa, young Stanley sang in a concert as - the boy soprano. A critic reviewing the performance wrote - " A strange hush came over the hall as the young artist began his recital. Make no mistake about it, much more will be heard about - Master Stanley Holloway".

In the 1920's Ernest Lough made his name for making the recording in a *lush* voice - "Oh for the wings, for the wings of a dove". Stanley sang "O dry those tears" but he wasn't asked to record it on the primitive equipment available. Stanley thought his voice had more of a contralto than soprano quality. Fame was to come much later in a different way, unlike rewards reaped by the angelic voices of Aled Jones in the 1980's or Anthony Way in the 1990's.

W.S. Gilbert had his *Sorcerer* - John Wellington Wells, changing people's lives with magic potions. Just for fun some parents may go to a fair and have the fortunes of members of the family read from a crystal ball. Others read up their signs of the zodiac in Old Moore's Almanac. Florrie and George Holloway had Stanley's bumps read and kept the list of predictions. After the laying on of hands, the curves on young Stanley's scalp revealed that 'he would have sympathy, be courageous but not be over physically strong. He would be ambitious, sociable, have a large willpower, love pets, reason well and know success at school. He will be fair at music, but better at drawing. He should be trained as a doctor or dentist!'

Some people today are inclined to take more than a passing interest in horoscopes. Others may feel any permutation of sayings applied to thousands of people are likely to show some points of significance for them. Stanley, born on 1st October, was a Libran.

What the balance of that sign, held for him, with hindsight we now know. Although Stanley wasn't very successful at school he could apparently draw. A career in medicine or dentistry didn't appeal to him. He certainly turned out to be very fair at music. Physically he did have to contend with the effects of asthma. Other aspects of the accuracy of these predictions we may recognise as we look at his life.

Ironically in years to come Stanley made a recording reading W.S. Gilbert's Bab Ballads. One was about phrenology. In this Sir Herbert White tells police sergeant James to arrest the man he has caught. Removing the rogue's cap, the sergeant recognises some significant bumps in the man's favour. One of these meant the owner was liable to practice innocent hilarity. If Stanley had such a bump the phrenologist must have missed it or maybe it only became more prominent later.

Stanley recalled hearing a barrel organ playing in the suburban streets around Forest Gate. When he was a boy it jingled out the popular tune - "Just a song at twilight when the lights are low and the flickering shadows softly come and go". Stanley was sometimes sent out to a street seller who rang a handbell and cried - "Muffins for sale!". The green baize covered tray, well balanced on the man's head, was lowered to supply muffins that were delicious when toasted for tea.

A school founded by the Worshipful Company of Carpenters was chosen for Stanley. It was far less crowded and had more status than the ordinary elementary school most children went to. Stanley sang in the school choir too until his voice broke. This can be a traumatic event for any boy and especially for one who has progressed enough to sing occasional solos. He was far from pleased when he unfortunately *dried up*. He was appropriately singing *"Oh rest in the Lord"* from Mendlessohn's oratorio *The Elijah*.

3

It is not easy for a boy to - "wait patiently for Him" but the words of that aria duly came true. "And he shall give thee thy heart's desire" was for Stanley, a new light baritone voice.

In a good Victorian home at the turn of the century, Stanley enjoyed reading the adventures of Sherlock Holmes. Arthur Conan Doyle was pressurised by his publishers to resurrect his mysterious detective living at 221B Baker Street. Queen Victoria's 64 years reign ended in 1901. Further Conan Doyle stories appeared in the Strand Magazine in October 1903. Doctor Watson was suitably surprised to recount - 'The Return'. Readers young and older were thrilled again by the exploits.

Stanley's father could sing and read bible lessons well in church. On his mother's side an uncle was a Shakespearean actor. Cousin Oliver was a theatrical agent. Uncle Bob was a useful influence because he was a self taught pianist who also sang comic songs. He gave Stanley a couple of songs to sing at parties. Stanley sang in talent concerts and was paid half a crown (12½p) per performance. He also appeared at the People's Palace known as the Drury Lane of the East End.

The Stratford Empire Music Hall was a local attraction and Stanley went there to watch with a friend, on Monday evenings. They experienced the thrill of seeing colourful acts. Marie Lloyd, George Lashwood and other famous stars played to full houses.

Young boys needed to enjoy some fresh air and sport. Stanley liked playing cricket. At the wicket in the park he could pretend to be W.G. Grace, the bearded legendary batsman who was nearing the end of his fine playing career. In county and test cricket for Gloucestershire and England for he scored over 54,000 runs.

The Holloways were proud owners of a piano. Stanley remembered his sister Millicent playing it. The piano had pride of place in the front room or parlour with an aspidistra plant.

4

Family, friends and guests without radio or television were more used to making their own entertainment. One of many popular songs of the day was - "Tell me pretty maiden are there any more at home like you?" This came from the American show *Floradora* by Leslie Stuart. The parent of a pupil friend heard Stanley fooling around, making fun of a serious song. He advised Stanley against this and asked him to practice with his very promising voice. The man invited Stanley to perform at a concert. 16 year old Master Holloway sang Sir Arthur Sullivan's "Lost Chord" at the Chelsea Town Hall in 1906.

To earn some money, a regular job of work was the next important step for Stanley. He was paid 10/- (50p) a week as a junior clerk at Messrs Everitts, Nutta and Jetta. He did not find employment at a boot polish factory very interesting. Stanley tried a season singing on the pier at Walton-on-the-Naze where he had so nearly drowned as a baby.

Tenors and ladies romantically savoured hearing "The English Rose" - sung by someone acting the part of Sir Walter Raleigh - "Dan cupid hath a garden and women are the flowers". This was from the show - Merrie England by Edward German which competed well with imported musicals. Stanley with his improving baritone voice was more suited to the role of the Earl of Essex with his dramatic number - "The Yeomen of England".

In 1909 George Holloway pointed out to his family in the newspaper that the Frenchman Louis Bleriot was the first person to fly across the English Channel. The shows of Offenbach, with notorious Can Can dancers, had already arrived and were very popular in London theatres. Might not similar invasions of European ideas be imported here more quickly in the future?

Young Stanley sang in a concert at Margate jetty. His pleasing voice was heard both in the morning singing - "Before the dawn", "The Better Land" and "Alone on a Raft".

5

In the afternoon his programme was varied with "Oh dry those tears" and "Beauties Eyes" by Tosti! One wonders if anyone planned a connection or if the choice was unintentional!

To help mother with the cost of living at home, after father had left them, Stanley tried another job. The secure work with a company at Billingsgate, he soon found was as equally boring as his first job. Both entailed book keeping and adding up long columns of figures. At least he was paid 5/- (25p) a week more. It meant he had to put up with the smell of fish instead of boot polish. After the first work experience he always kept his boots clean!

For interest and relaxation Stanley joined the London Rifle Brigade and enjoyed some shooting. He could also, with the raise, afford some singing lessons. Working with teacher Randall Jackson for 2/- (10p) per session, Stanley, with his rich voice, became more sought after to sing popular ballad songs.

The liveliest entertainment was to be found at the Music Halls. Stanley still went along when he could. He was enthralled by Marie Lloyd. She was known as the 'Queen of the Halls'. One song she sang was - "The boy I love is up in the gallery - there he is, can't you see? a waving his handkerchief". All the men waved their hankies furiously. She had such a magnetic personality she seemed to be singing to each one of them. Marie entertained audiences many of whom, on their small incomes, were often rather poorly clothed and undernourished. She brightened their lives with her lively, saucy suggestive songs.

Stanley when age 17 might easily have rubbed shoulders with Lenin! The young Russian was in London for the Social Democratic Congress in 1907 at Fulbourne Street, Limehouse. Lenin went to the Music Halls and wrote to Maxim Gorky "There are certain satirical sceptical attitudes towards the commonplace - there is an attempt to turn it inside out, to distrust somewhat and point out the illogicality of everyday things!".

This freely translated from the Russian defines satire but did he enjoy it at all!?

Stanley remembered going to the Tivoli theatre in the Strand. His ticket, some cigarettes, a meat pie and tram fare home cost just sixpence (2½p!). Returning happily homewards in the crowd, Stanley echoed with them again the fun they had hearing Lottie Collins singing "Ta ra da boom de ay". While such shows were beneath the dignity of many middle class people, there were observers of the times who made perceptive notes in their diaries. The author Rudyard Kipling went to Gattis at Charing Cross. He wrote - Music Halls supply a gap in the national history and people have not yet realised how much they have to do with national life". Also in the poem 'Tommy' he showed how the common soldier was treated. A trooper belonged in the gallery seats or music halls but when there was fighting to be done his place was in the stalls of theatres of war.

From his pulpit an East End clergyman said "There probably was a place for Music Halls in everyday life". He was called before the Bishop to account for his outrageous comments. The priest called Marie Lloyd as a witness. When asked to comment about music hall entertainment being unacceptable she said "My Lord, it is all in the minds of members of the audience". As an example she sang a song well known to him and enjoyed in many respectable drawing rooms. Hitching up her skirt and beckoning suggestively - she invited the audience to "Come into the garden Maud!". They were surprised a song could convey meanings to people, very different from those intended.

Marie Lloyd

Stanley was sacked for being disinterested in his office work.He took a risk and relying on his stage of experience he turned to   working as an entertainer. This was a precarious step as income from this source was uncertain. He joined Wilson James White Coons Concert Party at the pier at Walton-on-the-Naze. He tried a different *deep end* when auditioning for Will Pepper. Accepted, Stanley was kitted out from head to toe with a costume white suit with bobbles, matching white cap and boots.

As a pierrot Stanley received £3 a week. For two months entertained holidaymakers. He learned a lot about being in front of audiences including how to please them and react to occasional indifference. Joining in and helping the troupe with anything at a moment's notice, was a useful part of his apprenticeship. He was a utility man acting any part in sketches from policeman to bus conductor. As a concessional treat he was allowed to drive the electric tram 1½ miles along the pier. A popular song summed up people's feelings - "You can do a lot of things at the seaside that you can't do in town!"

Stanley remembered the names of many seaside concert parties that moved around and performed at the resorts:- Scamps, Brownies, Fol de Rols, Scarlet Mysteries, Tatlers, Vagabonds etc. etc. Each had five or six members with different talents. They clowned and sang with unpretentious material and very little capital money, amusing the trippers.

Songwriters were beginning to get a fairer return for their skill, sometimes with contracts if music and libretti were used in theatres. Up to then they may have only been paid a pound for a piece music and others could make much more from it. Stanley said artists tried out new songs and if they proved popular they were fully exploited by   writer and artist registering a copyright.

One of the problems of being a touring artist is finding good lodgings.

Stanley recalled with amusement an incident when staying at Mrs. Hodge's tidy guest house. A colleague of his, Arthur Riscoe, told the landlady the toilet cistern was difficult to manage. She advised him to "surprise it to make it work!". Mr. Hodge used to take out some dried chicken bones, strung together. He waved them around the head of the actors staying there and chanted an incantation as a seance medium. Like the zodiac, fortune tellers and phrenologists, appealed to mystic powers for good fortune on the work of the entertainer.

CHAPTER TWO

Marriage, Italy and the First World War.

Stanley bought a buttonhole flag for the National Lifeboat Institution funds, in the summer of 1913 on Clacton pier. He was twenty three years old. The previous year the 46,000 ton White Star liner Titanic, which was thought to be unsinkable, had left Britain on her maiden voyage to America. On 14th April, Titanic hit an iceberg and sank. Over 1,500 men, women and children were drowned in freezing waters of the north Atlantic ocean. Clearly the memory of this disaster was still in some people's minds when they saw the sea. The loss of so many loved ones, evoked the sympathy of those not directly involved.

The young brunette Alice Mary Laure Foran, known to her friends as Queenie, reacted to Stanley's banter as he posted some coins into the collecting tin. "Getting to know you" is the next stage of courting, as Rogers and Hammerstein so ably expressed much later in their musical *The King and I*. On dates, during the next few weeks Stanley and Queenie ate ice cream cornets together, walked on the pier or drank tea.

9

"LOVE, love changes everything, nothing in the world can ever be the same". What each individual knows or understands of this emotion has been expressed over the years in music from Grand Opera to the popular musical shows and songs today. The fulfilment of natural feelings and social behaviour of maturing adults goes on. We all know of seemingly incongruous partnerships which sometimes result from chance meetings in unusual places. Romance can be fuelled by parental expectations or individual fear of solitude. More significant factors of compatability and religion may be considered at leisure. Love is the driving force for most people deciding to get married.

One of the biggest decisions of our lives, to get married or not, is often made under some pressure and at risk of loss. Any prospect of a higher income for Stanley at this time would have been very welcome. He was billed as a light baritone and performed at the prestigious Westcliff Gardens at Clacton-on-sea. He had enjoyed three good seasons with Graham Russell and Bentley's concert party. At the end of the summer of 1913, Stanley saw the great Harry Lauder topping the bill at the Tivoli in the Strand. Leslie Henson, when visiting his mother at Clacton saw Stanley perform. He thought Stanley showed promise and offered him a place in a touring show called *Nicely Thanks*.

In November 1913 Stanley took yet another plunge on the Essex coast, he was married. *'Til death us do part'* was vowed at St. James Church, Clacton, next to the famous gardens. The honeymoon was spent at the Great Eastern hotel at Liverpool Street station. From there Stanley could attend rehearsals for Leslie Henson's show. Queenie and Stanley set up home at 'Gunville', Ellis Road, Clacton. Queenie was an orphan but had a small regular income from the ground rent of London property which she had inherited. Stanley was then earning £4. 10 shillings a week. The weekly cost of renting the house was 15/- (75p).

10

By 1913, the British were becoming accustomed to travelling by train. Railway tracks radiated out from the hubs of London, the industrial midlands and northern cities. This made seaside resorts more easily accessible for holidays and day trips. Bathing machines, huts on wheels providing separate facilities for men and women to change into long modest costumes, stood in shallow water. Children laughed at the antics of Punch and Judy, portrayed in a striped portable puppet theatre erected on the sandy beaches. Many more boarding houses and hotels became established to cope with the visitors. People on holiday left their cares behind in the noisy, dirty mills and factories.

"Oh I do like to be beside the seaside" they sang and wanted entertainment whatever the weather. Therefore pier shows, pierrot troupes on the front and theatres were increasingly in demand and Stanley secured regular seasonal employment.

The following Spring of 1914 Stanley, with the suggestion and help of a friend, took the opportunity to go to Italy for singing lessons. Maestro Signor Fernandino, at Via Montabello in Milan asked him to sing. Stanley couldn't understand or speak Italian. Responding to a gesture to begin, Stanley nearly broke into one of his popular baritone songs from his concert repertoire. 'Boots' by Kipling and McCall would have made him less nervous and remind him of his first work at the boot polish factory. Fortunately however, another student there could interpret and explain to him that he should show the range and timbre of his voice in an arpeggio. When the puzzled Stanley heard the word *scales*, with a sigh of relief he showed Signor Fernandino what he could do.

In Milan, perhaps Stanley didn't have the time, money or opportunity to go to La Scala and listen to world famous baritones he admired. Stanley was told he had a promising and pleasing voice. In six months the resonance and projection had improved considerably.

11

Signor Fernandino his teacher, was very disappointed to hear that Stanley had decided to return to England and continue a career in lighter entertainment.

When he returned home, Stanley signed up with another pierrot troupe called the Grotesques. After a while they were booked to go on an overseas tour to South America. Before he left on this trip, the Holloway's first child, Joan, was born on 1st October, Stanley's own birthday. This was the finest present any proud father could have wished for. Stanley remembered rushing off at three o'clock in the morning to fetch the doctor. He had to ride hurriedly there and back on a bicycle without a headlamp.

In 1914, there was news about Fernandino - not Stanley's singing teacher but the Archduke Ferdinand, who was assassinated at Sarajevo on August 4th. At this time, British workers and families were filling their lungs with ozone, enjoying all the fun of a seaside holiday and watching concert parties.

Stanley set off for South America taking a second class berth on a mail steamer. On arrival at Buenos Aires in Brazil he heard that the famous singer Caruso and Madame Tetrazzini (the leading soprano from Covent Garden opera) were performing in the city. Gracie Fields later told Stanley how Madame Tetrazzini had come to hear her singing in variety. Madame requested that Gracie sing a straight, non- comical song. On hearing Gracie's voice, Madame Tetrazzini said she wished her own highest notes were as clear and secure. Gracie, like Stanley, had settled for a career in lighter entertainment

Stanley was paid £5 per week to be in the show at the Colon theatre with the Los Grotesquos, as his group were known. It amused him that HOY on the billboard outside meant tonight!. One evening Stanley peeped through the spyhole in the curtain to see how many were seated in the audience. He saw the unmistakable figure in a white shirt.

The maestro Enrico Caruso was there relaxing from his operatic exertions. At the end of his act Stanley duly obliged with a hurriedly chosen encore. Jack Granville his accompanist began and Stanley sang "Take thou this rose", a popular drawing room ballad in Edwardian England. The famous tenor was seen warmly applauding the piece and Stanley only realised later that the song was in Caruso's own repertoire.

Some amusing incidents on the tour Stanley remembered were connected with V. Foster. Vivian Foster was styled the Clerical Comic. Foster used to say his father worked for a newspaper and he was the first *addition*. Stanley later recalled a shocking story involving a tango melody called "El Chocolo", popular at tea dances. (The Grotesques' pianist played the tune in an improvised medley). Fred Emney, a comedian friend told Stanley - "As pianist I was playing in variety in Mexico. A customer asked me to play "El Chocolo". When I refused the Mexican took out his revolver and fired three shots into the piano. Naturally I then played "El Chocolo" as requested until dawn!". A risky business, being an entertainer!

The concert party moved to another booking at Valparaiso in Chile. News had reached the company of war raging in the trenches on the Western Front. Stanley felt rather guilty at not being at home near his wife and family or doing something in the struggle against the Kaiser. When Los Grostesquos reached Iquique in northern Chile, Stanley planned to secretly leave the troupe and return home. When his intention was discovered he agreed to stay one more week whilst an understudy was trained to take over his parts.

For £60, which was a lot of money in those days, Stanley paid his passage on a   3,000 ton mail steamer back to Liverpool. From Lime Street station to London and on to Clacton didn't take as long. Leslie Henson met Stanley and wanted him to take a juvenile lead part at the Gaiety theatre. Though Stanley very much wanted opportunities in the theatre, as a young

13

man, aged 25, like so many other young men then, he was keen to join the army and do his bit. There were unavoidable compelling posters everywhere, pointing and saying - Kitchener Wants You! Leslie Henson was rather irritated to have his advice ignored but had to accept Stanley's patriotic aim to get into the army as quickly as possible.

Army regiments were distinctive with name and badge proudly boasting famous battles. Most county names had been present at confrontations dating back to Waterloo. Stanley told the recruiting officer of of his experience in London Rifle Brigade. With some further help from a serving man, Stanley joined the Connaught Rangers. He was recruited into the Irish regiment and bought a commission. After basic officer training he was sent as a second lieutenant not to France, but to Cork in southern Eire. His first taste of action was not against Germans but Irish who rebelled in Dublin in 1916.

In O'Connell Street, the Post Office had been commandeered by Sinn Feiners singing "Die wacht am Rhein". In spite of appeals by the Governor, Sir Matthew Natham, they barricaded themselves in to establish their protests. Stanley was sent with a company and some 2,000 troops to besiege them and restore Law and Order. The Easter Rising lasted for six days. One of the youths with field ambulances helping carry away the wounded on stretchers wrote about his experiences. He was the son of the Postmaster Mr. Norway and his speech was impeded by a marked stammer.

The Connaught Rangers were posted to France. They joined the 16th Irish Division, veterans of the Somme battle, where Haig's men were mown down in hundreds of thousands by enemy machine guns. Stanley remembered being in some fighting at Wyschaete Ridge but like most soldiers, was reticent to talk about it. Bombardment by heavy shelling in Flanders is something survivors didn't want to be reminded of.

14

Stanley admitted being very frightened at times by the enormous noise. He had suffered from a scaley skin condition called psoriasis and also from asthma. The Medical Officer planned to send him home for treatment. However, as Stanley's Commanding Officer knew his lieutenant had been an entertainer in civilian life, he ordered Stanley to organise shows to raise the morale of the shattered troops.

Lieutenant. S.A. Holloway

The men returned daily - tired, hungry, scared and dispirited from futile turns of duty. One of the men in their unit had been awarded the Victoria Cross for exceptional gallantry. A show to cheer the men up and commemorate this event was called *Wear that ribbon*. Surprisingly talented new acquaintances from among the serving men, came forward to help fill a programme of Stanley's first effort as producer. Godfrey Tearle, Vernon Castle, Eric Blore, Edmund Gwen and Stanley acted and sang, inviting participation in choruses of well known songs. Soldiers were reminded of better times and home. Company commanders noted the uplifting effect, and reported it back to headquarters (with the other mostly negative depressing information about more enormous numbers of killed and wounded).

Harold Walding, my father, served with the Royal Horse Guards in 1915 and fought in the trenches in France. He was pleased by the shows and later copied Stanley Holloway's song "My Old Dutch" and the Street Watchman's monologue story. These eased the fearful sounds of machine gunfire and after a barrage, the dreaded order to go "Over the top!". Dad was

15

wounded and repatriated for treatment. He learned to recite the Charles Winter monologue:-

"Some chaps gets the fat and some chaps gets the lean when they start on their journey thro'

life. Some makes pots of money at being M.P.'s and some gets it by taking a wife.

Some learns a good trade such as Dustman or Sweep, which the same I'd have done if

I'd knowed, but the special profession I've drifted to now is 'Minding a 'ole in the road".

This yarn painted a picture of ordinary road works in a London street near dad's home in

Hackney. He was married on leave. He had to go back to France and crawl and wade through

flooded shell crater holes at the front line again before the armistice in 1918.

Stanley was repatriated and stationed in county Durham. He was a demobilised after

being with a Yorkshire regiment. He heard plenty of that dialect and the Irish of his

colleagues. Stanley sang at the Empire theatre, Hartlepool, and several times heard Ernest

Hastings recite two monologues by Weston and Lee - "And yet I don't know" and "My word

you do look queer".

When free of uniform at last, Stanley hurried south to Clacton in his civilian clothes .

In the army, Stanley had converted from being a protestant to catholicism, to meet with his

wife's wishes that their children be bought up in that faith. Daughter Joan was growing

nicely and was known by a nickname, Paddy.

Corporal Walding was repatriated and demobilised, still carrying a piece of shrapnel in his

arm muscle which doctors then thought too risky to remove. After the war, mum and dad set

up home in Cricklewood. The holes in the road from zeppelin bombers had all been filled.

Our family of six moved out to Luton in 1938 and dad still did his party pieces at concerts.

One of these much later was to celebrate their ruby wedding when he sang "My old Dutch".

16

Dad collected lots of 12 inch 78 speed wax records and played them at home. I remember hearing some of various music hall artists, singing and reciting, including one of Stanley's fine version of "My Old Dutch. (Some damaged records were shaped into flower bowls in wartime by immersing them in hot water). My father's birth certificate, which I found accidently amongst his papers, gave information about the grandfather I never knew. It showed my grandfather's job as foreman at a boot factory at Hackney in east London. Could it, I wonder, have been the one where Stanley started his working life?

Stanley showed an interest in good footballers, as many men do. In 1913 the Football Association Challenge Cup Final was played before 120,000 fans packed into the Crystal Palace stadium. After ninety minutes of play, Aston Villa in their claret coloured jerseys and baggy shorts had scored once to win the cup over Sunderland playing in red and white.

It was very important for Stanley quickly resume working life in the theatre. Summer seasons at the seaside were short and insecure. London or a another big city were the places to be. He could earn a more reliable income by being in all year round shows. Progress was fairly slow for most hopeful stars and entertainment was not fully recognised as a profession. Being in M.H.A.R.A. helped because the Music Hall Railway Artists Association members paid half price concessional fares on the railways.

Where was the natural place for Stanley to find lodgings in London close to his work? *A flat in Holloway Road!* (also a low note in the baritone register!). Stanley remembered his talented friend and mentor, Leslie Henson, was impressively dressed when he arrived in Clacton to see Stanley in a show. Henson wore a smart fashionable trilby hat with spats over his shoes and twirled an embossed cane. Henson took Stanley off for an audition.

By 1918, those men still interested in football remembered the other cruel contest they

17

were recently involved in. Some of the khaki tunics had been stained red with stripes of

blood and men had fallen in the poppy fields of Flanders. They had strived to win for their

captain Field Marshall Haig but it had proved to be a costly match. Stanley's unit lost many

brave men and dad some good friends. The survivors now sought success in peacetime.

CHAPTER THREE

Treading the boards.

Kissing Time was the first show in which Stanley appeared, after his audition with

Felix Edwards. The show ran at the Winter Gardens, Drury Lane, formerly known as the

Middlesex Music hall, from the 20th May, 1919 for 439 performances. The story was

adapted from a French one - Madame et son Filleul (godson), by P.G. Wodehouse and Guy

Bolton with music by Ivan Carlisle. The title chosen, accidentally or on purpose, was the

same as one of the hit songs in the record breaking *Chu Chin Chow.*

Kissing Time - the PLOT is set in
Georgette's villa. There is confusion
among characters after an exchange of
identity papers.

CAST: Leslie Henson - Bibi St. Fol
(A chauffeur who doubles as cook to
the 33rd Company of the regiment.)

Leslie Henson

The supporting cast are:- George Grossmith - Max Touquet, George Barrett - Brichoux

Phyllis Dare - Lucienne Touquet, Stanley Holloway - Captain Wentworth.

Leslie Henson was a much loved character by audiences and critics.

Sometimes when George Grossmith and the first understudy were indisposed Stanley, who could learn quickly, took over the leading role of Max Touquet. Theatre proprietors and impresarios look for the next show almost as soon as the present one is on. They know audiences have to be kept interested in styles and actors if they are to return again for more.

A Night Out, at the same theatre, saw Stanley cast in another musical comedy part. The show was produced by Charles Froman and George Edwards in 1920 and ran for 300 performances. As a result, these two men went on to arrange other shows together.

PLOT: Rene, a struggling French sculptor hopes to achieve fame and fortune with his creation when it is exhibited shortly in Paris. The scene alternates between studio and Hotel Pimlico. In a fracas with the police, Pinglett knocks out seven constables before he is knocked unconscious by a policewoman. At the court of justice the summons is quashed.

CAST: Joseph Pinglett - Leslie Henson,   Maxime   - Austin Melford

Lily St John   - Phyllis Monkman   Victorine   - Elsa Macfarlane

Rene   - Stanley Holloway.

A critic in Fragments, the theatre

magazine, writes -

"Rene creates the model of a lady,

clad even more lightly than in the

prevailing fashion". It seems from

this the shackles of Victorian

restraint were slowly being

loosened in the Edwardian theatre.

Movement towards free expression in this country was slow for another forty years.

This small part was another progressive experience for Stanley. He recalled later in a radio interview, a catchy musical chorus about the "Hotel Pimli, Pimli Pimli, hotel Pimlico".

In amusing 1920's repartee, Austin Melford, as Maxime, finds a door locked and putting his ear to the keyhole he asks "Is there anyone there?" To a surprising gruff reply from Leslie Henson - "No only the furniture", dull witted Maxime continues - "You sound rather hoarse". Henson's punch line is "Yes, I'm a *horse* hair sofa!".

It was during a performance of *A Night Out* that the second child for the Holloways, John, was born. It was and is not at all easy for married people being in show business if they have to travel to performances and have young children. Stanley toured around using temporary accommodation and returned, going home to his wife Queenie, whenever he could. A settled home is needed for upbringing and schooling and although Stanley couldn't share in it as fully as he would have wished, at least the family had a secure base at Clacton.

Infrequently, Stanley's whole family could sit together in the parlour wearing the new fangled headphones. The National Telephone Company hired out four receivers for £10 per year. As a precursor to radio, various short spoken or musical programmes could be heard .

The cast performing at the Winter Garden theatre in the Spring of 1921, had a discussion about their future. Leslie Henson was alright for with his talent and fame, he had further bookings. In his opinion however, the farcical musical comedy they were in would probably end in June. With two million people unemployed everybody was being as economical as they could and this diminished the prospects of successful shows. Having no prospects at all Stanley remembered his happy times at seaside concert parties. One evening he said "Wouldn't it be fun if a few of us took some small props in cars?

We could do one night stands touring around coastal resorts, until something else turns up?"

Davy Burnaby chipped in "Why not do that in London?". Davy Burnaby was something of a

specialist in concert party work. He had been educated at Pembroke College, Cambridge,

after attending Haileybury Public School. One end of term school report was taken home to

the vicarage and his clergyman father. The English master had enjoyed Davy's performance

in the school concert and wrote "Shows promise as an actor" Davy went on to gain valuable

experience working in the Cambridge University - *Footlights Revue shows.* An under-

graduate friend of his, Philip Braham, wrote "Limehouse Blues". This proved popular and

successful at that time. Davy had gone on to tour for three years, in open air pavilions, with

The March Hares. He was now very practical and could turn his hand to anything in theatre

even writing a song for the Caldicott twins.

The possibility of forming a concert party was enhanced by cast members' reminiscences

of their experience in France. A concert was organised at Wimereux in 1919 to cheer up the

occupying regular peace time troops. The soldiers had the unenviable task of keeping a

watch on the Rhine and any possible German armament activities. Leslie Henson,

Eric Blore, Jack Buchanan and Stanley remembered being in an insolent sketch called

"The Disorderly Room". Tired soldiers were sent into fits of laughter when a parody was

made of battalion headquarters. The soldiers saw the most important papers for

postings, promotions, leave, repatriation and   demobilisation being mismanaged in a

chaotic way. Jack Buchanan had been purposely plied with extra drinks before the show.

Exceptionally for him with his high stage reputation, he was seen to fall down.

Laddie Cliff, Gilbert Childs, Binnie Hale, Phyllis Dare and Elsa Macfarlane remembered

this and other pranks and how they pleased the troops with their song and dance routines.

Those discussing this show now also remembered that a pianist, Jackson Hylton, was only just in time at Victoria station to catch the boat train to Dover. As his reputation grew he was billed as Jack Hylton.

Over a meal with friends in the Cavour restaurant in Leicester Square, Stanley met Davy Burnaby sounding out Laddie Cliff as a possible producer for their concert party idea. Archie de Bear, who ran his own show *R.S.V.P.* at Southsea, seemed very interested in the project. Once in Hampshire, someone in the cast pointed out to him not everyone audience perhaps knew what *R.S.V.P.* stood for? Archie's reply was "Well tell them it means *Reaches Southsea Via Portsmouth!.*"

For anyone to break into the London theatre scene in 1921 would not be easy. *Chu Chin Chow* still dominated box office sales. A record was reached when over 2.8 million people saw it at His Majesty's theatre. It had run from 1916 for six nights a week with matinees on Wednesday, Thursday and Saturday. One critic said "It was the most underdressed overdressed show in town." However as newspaper and delivery boys worked on cold rainy days they bravely whistled - "We are the robbers of the wood" and felt better. Others in romantic mood agreed - "Any time's kissing time". Another rival for its share of audiences was Fraser Simpson's *The Maid of the Mountains* It ran at Daly's theatre. Edwardian couples hoped "A paradise for two" would be theirs. At that time to sing a "Bachelor Gay" was unquestionably very acceptable not posing a threat to society.

New ideas would have also to compete with shows called *revues* which were attracting increasing audiences. Archie de Bear, Laddie Cliff and Davy Burnaby began to work out the structure of the proposed new group. Betty Chester was one of ladies in the cast prepared to make a commitment. She was a friend of a talented young artist/writer/producer Noel

22

Coward. She appeared with him in *The knight of the Burning Pestle*. Betty had a fine

contralto voice and had sung in musical comedies. Another, Phyllis Monkman, was an

attractive dancer and singer with experience at the Alhambra theatre. She wanted to join the

party. Bab's Valerie was a useful addition as a promising utility artiste.

The necessary capital money was raised, Archie de Bear invested £250, Laddie Cliff was

prepared to put £400 into his production. Clifford Whitely, a journalist, joined the company

management team to look after the interests of £250 invested by an unknown Mr. Brown.

Leslie Henson could not be persuaded to put up £100. The syndicate expected a proportional

return on their capital. Four key performers would to collect £50 per week plus 10% of any

profits. Others, including Stanley and the stage manager Stanley Brightman expected to be

paid £25 a week which was very acceptable. Summing up, Laddie Cliff said of their

prospects "We've three pioneers and two pianners, that's all!".

Davy Burnaby, with his drive and influential friends at the golf club, was recognised as

being very responsible for founding the troupe. Later in retirement, Stanley referred to

Burnaby as "Dear old Davy, the father, the uncle, the host, the fat genial co-op of Co-Ops.

The Anti-Wasters i.e. economists was suggested as a name. Archie de Bear thought *The*

Co-Optimists was a better catchy attractive title. This was agreed and for the opening chorus

number they sang with heart and voice - "Optimists are we wherever we may go,

though we may be short of money life for us is always sunny".

Purple and Gold coloured cotton pierrot costumes were made with ruffle collars and

bobbles, with matching silk skull caps. For scenery white trellice pillars were capped with

leafy laurel plants. The original production set was by Hugh Willoughby. He had designed

sets and dresses when a prisoner of war in Holland. Theatre historian Ernest Short wrote:-

23

"For only £300, this was a triumphant demonstration of economy and value from ingenuity and wit, as opposed to mere money". Two pianos for accompanists Melville Gideon and Harry Pepper, were bought on hire purchase. Rehearsals began at the vacant Lyric theatre in Shaftesbury Avenue. Archie de Bear negotiated with his friend de Courville for the use of the Royalty theatre. A show *Pins and Needles* came to an end prematurely after only a five week run. For a rental of £100 per week *The Co-Optimists* had a home base.

Optimists they certainly needed to be to step out and succeed in the very competitive world of entertainment. The members of the troupe were good friends on and off stage. They were raring to go like the horse *Humorist*, which bravely accepted the challenge and sprinted over the turf at Epsom to win the Derby. Perhaps this was a good omen for their show.

CHAPTER FOUR

Co-Optimism movement. Pierrots are in town.

The Co-Optimists show opened at the Royalty Theatre, Kingsway on 27th June, 1921.

The heat that summer in the streets was sweltering. Though on warm evenings it was

unreasonable to expect people to flock into even warmer theatres without air conditioning,

they surprisingly did. Night after night most seats were sold. The inexplicable chemistry of

artists, talents, solo and ensemble song, dance, programme order and troupe costumes

had somehow created a winner. An aptly named fun sketch 'A Midsummer Night's Scream'

didn't turn out to be a real nightmare!

The well rehearsed show was seen by large audiences. The programme began with the

whole company on stage singing the opening chorus "Co-Optimists are we".

In turn a spotlight picked out each member who introduced themself. Davy Burnaby, first, as

a kind of chairman explained the Synopsis -

"Sin is to do wrong and opis what they

make the beer from!"

Davy and each member in turn sang:-

"Hello everybody I'm the fat one of

the group, they're going to carve me up

one day to make another troupe, I hope my

confidential talk enthusiasm rouses, I've

sung before The Duke of York and other -

public houses!".

Davy Burnaby

The chorus then all sang "Bow-Wow!" and made some general funny comment:

"I'm Melville Gideon as all of you must know, I'm the most important person in this little show, they cannot do without me as you can plainly see, where're they go they're bound to be accompanied by me - Bow-Wow!".

"My name is Harry Pepper which you need not be surprised, at for I play all the twiddly bits that Melville Gideon shies at - Bow-Wow - you cad!".

Laddie Cliff

"Now I am little Laddie and I think you'll all agree, there's no one in the show who's half as good as me, I'm going to sing a song or two that goes with lots of bits, I once sang down at Dover and they pushed me off the cliff!   Bow-Wow - shut up!".

"Now I am Phyllis Monkman and I'm always on the go, I deputise for all the talking stars lately don't you know, but lately on the wireless I've been busy as a bee, when you heard the nightingale you little thought 'twas me Bow-Wow".

(An early broadcasting innovation was the use of an outside microphone to relay a nightingale's song nightingale directly from Berkeley Square.)

"I'm Peggy Petronella, so hello how d'ye do, I play all the tiniest parts they don't want to do".

Stanley Holloway came into the spotlight. Several well known trade marks and a steam laundry included the name "Holloway". There was also the the infamous Women's prison, in north London and Holloway Road station on the railway. Stanley didn't mention his name.

" I'll sing a song of sixpence like
the famous Woolworth's store, I'll
sing of fourteen shillings, five
and nine * and two and four, I'm
famous on the gramophone my name is
always starred, the police have all
my records in a book at Scotland
Yard   Bow-Wow - It's nice!"
As an alternative opening Stanley
some-times sang:-

Stanley Holloway

"My name is one you can't forget, your memory cannot fail, you've only got to think of pills,
ointment, gin and jail!".

On the original programme at the Royalty, Stanley sang - "The wind in the trees". He
was also in sketches entitled - 'Operatic Golf', - 'Choosing a test team', - 'Ronux' and -
'Full dog Gerald', a parody on the famous exploits of the popular fictional character -
Bulldog Drummond by Sapper (the nom de plume for H.C. McNeile). One of Sapper's avant
garde adventures combined the topical ideas of progress in airship construction and poison
gas as a threat (from experience in the last war).

"Hello everybody though no-one cares a hang, my name is Miss Macfarlane
so I won't detain you *lang*, my other name is Elsa and I'd shout hip hip hurray, if
I only had a song to sing or *else a* part to play. Bow-Wow   ooh er!"

(* old sterling money 6d, 14/- 5/9d and 2/4d)

27

"Now I am Betty Chester, I am also on
on the list, you'll find I'll co-op about
for this   Co-Optimist, I'm certain as a
vocalist that I shall be the best, I can
get notes off my *chest a* little lower
than the rest- Bow-Wow I'll be there!"
  "To be a humble comic is my melacholy
fate, though I had ambitions to be a

Betty Chester

plumbers mate, I'm one of Mrs Child's twins the fact I'll proudly tell, I'm

Gilbert Childs

pleased to say that both mother and
childs are doing well! - Bow-Wow - oh gosh!"
Parody and satire were becoming more
acceptable as an approach to comedy and
even comments about royalty were included.
In Music Hall and a Gilbert and Sullivan
show, anomalies in behaviour of members
of society, were expressed from a critical but humorous
viewpoint. Royalty, the Church, the Army
and asthetes like Oscar Wilde were all parodied
One such new song was written by Greatrix Newman
and Wolseley Charles.

Stanley sang about a king wanting jam for tea! It was a subtle way of attacking the new laws
for early closing days, which gave shopkeepers a much needed midweek break.

In the song, to buy his favourite jam, the king goes out in the rain with an umbrella and wearing carpet slippers, not shoes. When his majesty finds the shop shut in midweek daytime he says - "I'll learn to sing the Red Flag and throw my crown into the sea!".

The public were fascinated by the news from Egypt in 1922, of the discovery of the tomb of Tutenkhamen. Howard Carter had made magnificent finds in the Valley of Kings by the river Nile. People were intrigued and speculated that Lord Caernarvon's mysterious death soon afterwards was in some way connected with a very old curse made on grave robbers. In a topical reaction, the *Co-Optimists* devised a 'burlesque' scene for their show. The term 'Burlesque' was used more widely in America where it meant 'to mock everyday things'. On stage for the *Co-Ops* Davy Burnaby was Queen Cleopatra and watched Egyptian treasures being removed. Members of the troupe suitably attired, solemnly processed past a throne carrying outrageously large replicas of:- an alarm clock, bottle of beer, book of old jokes, a string of sausages and the three brass balls of a pawnbrokers sign!.

2 L O was the name given to the first radio broadcasting station. The *Co-Optimists* were asked to perform over the air. Using early microphones, Stanley's voice and those of other members of the troupe were heard in many homes. Broadcasting was helping to open up the world with faster communication. Since the first successful transmission of sound across the Atlantic by Marconi in 1901, radio had been developed for domestic use. New receivers made by Marconiphone with two valves, were a great improvement over the first crystal or *cats' whiskers* sets, as they were called.

George Bernard Shaw had written a play called *Major Barbara*. W.S. Gilbert's philosophy that nothing can escape satire or parody if it is well intended, was *co-opted.*

Betty Chester explained the story line in her sonorous tones while the company paraded. On stage they resembled a Salvation Army band!. The sketch was called 'The Bandsman's Daughter!'. Stanley helped them keep in step by thumping on a big bass drum.

'Great Stuff this Education - a harrowing episode!", was a sketch written by Stanley Holloway and Davy Burnaby. They both appeared in it and *school* was deliberately used by the actors to appear ignorant about what everyone knew was a *college!* (Thank goodness the bursar at Harrow later didn't know of this or he might not have agreed to register Julian, Stanley's son, for admission in 1944!)

Members of the audience at the Prince of Wales Theatre in 1922 saw a Pierrotic Entertainment as the *Co-Optimists* performance styled themselves. Andre Charlot, the impresario, agreed to manage their show. After six weeks in the previous summer at the Royalty, the Co-Ops transferred to the Palace in the autumn of 1921, for 500 performances. Though the first shows were well attended, the running costs were not met by ticket sales and £5,000 was lost. The Co-Optimists' board of management thought the format needed changing. Davy Burnaby and Stanley disagreed. Charlot managed two successful seasons for them during which they played 232 and 210 record breaking shows.

Stanley sang a song about a "Cobbler", presumably not related to the most famous one in *Chu Chin Chow*. It proved a fairly popular ballad. The whole troupe then did a sketch 'Slay it with music'. After the interval, pierrot costumes were changed by the cast. In the second half of the show they dressed differently for their individual contributions. Scenes had to be changed quickly. - 'Stanley Holloway will try his voice', meant things could be rearranged while he sang in front of the curtain and continuity was ensured.

Poking fun at the popular fashionable well attended sport of horse racing was fair game and

30

the men in the troupe did a scene called 'The Junior Turf'.

J.B. Priestly had written his book 'The Good Companions'. People were interested to know what artists were like offstage and in private life. The *Co-Ops* did their 'Learningham Repertory Company', portraying (and humorously distorting further) impossible relationships between a producer and his cast. The subject still intrigues people who would like to know what famous actors and actresses are really like. Alan Ayckbourn much later with *A Chorus of Disapproval* and Michael Frayn with *Noises Off*, explore the theme more seriously employing the 'play within a play' dramatic device used by Shakespeare.

Old theatre programmes give useful information about prices and commodities of long ago. Men saw Army Club cigarettes rise in price to 1/- (5p) for twenty while ladies wondered if they could afford the new style cami knickers from Debenham and Freebody at 39/6d (£2). Other famous London department stores like Liberty's of Regent Street illustrated blouses in silk with fashionable tyrian collar and cuffs of net embroidery at 29/6d (£1.50d).
The black satin shoes as worn in the show by Miss Elsa Macfarlane could be purchased after the matinee at H. & M. Payne in Rupert Street for a mere 45 shillings (£2.25p.).

Some other practical imaginative publicity ideas crept into programmes. For the *Co-Ops* show at His Majesty's an attractive page gave the words of a catchy new song - "The more we are together the merrier we'll be". The words were headed A.O.F.B. and overprinted on an outline of a tankard. Legible in the froth was a request -
"To be kept until the end of the performance" when full copies of the words and music of The anthem of the Ancient Order of Froth Blowers" will be on sale by attendants!.

Ramsay Macdonald M.P. broke the monopoly of Liberals and Conservatives in Parliament. Watching this turn of events everyone wondered what effects it would have.

Neither Stanley nor Savoyards could now honestly sing from Gilbert and Sullivan's *Iolanthe* -"That every boy and every gal that's born into this world alive, is either a little Liberal or else a little Conservative tra la la!". Future fairy members of parliament like young Strephon would not just be Whigs or Tory's! The *Co-Optimists* show went to Birmingham in 1924. At the hippodrome there in June, Stanley was in a Dickensian fantasy -

"Bill and Oliver". With Gilbert Childs, Stanley sang a popular French song "Alouette", the audience joined in heartily with the chorus. Lady members of the cast were not as permanent as most men. New members:- Margery Spiers, Shelia Rawle, Doris Bentley, and Mary Lee joined the company. The only new man was Austin Melford. Stanley had worked with him in *A Night Out* when Austin got some good laughs in his role as the *dim* - Maxime!. In theatre at that time several members might move on to a new show together. Several of the cast of *Kissing Time* including Stanley, brought their talents to the new *Co-Optimists.*

Audiences, (because they buy the tickets) and critics, (because it is their job), express their feelings about shows. A critic in The Stage Magazine was dissatisfied for a time with the *Co-Ops* entertainment. He or she thought that - "The troupe might be called the only authentic follow on of the standard set by Harry Pelissier and his never to be forgotten *Follies.* It was thought the *Co-Ops* were worthy enough to run beside that famous troupe of super pierrots. It is all the more to be regretted how disappointing the first performance was. The re-produced company on 1st May, 1925 scarcely revived the old traditions. Much of the old snap and sparkle was missing and there were times when the performance came perilously near to being actually dull. It is difficult to account for such things, with such clever performers, authors and composers at hand. Perhaps what was most missing last evening - which should be considerably improved by now - was that indefinable quality

32

we call *atmosphere*. It may be too, that there was a little too much refinement in the air, although of course one would never accuse the *Co-Optimists* of *refanement!* A little more of the broader music-hall element emerging from the silk and satin of the pierrot would, however, be an advantage. The first half of the performance did not really come to life until Marriott Edgar dealt in lurid *'Lancasheer'* with King John signing the Magna Charta among the trippers' and shrimps at Runnymede. This funny performance brings to mind those in a similar vein by Stanley Holloway, but of course Mr. Edgar is the creator of these things."

This last comment shows Stanley was not involved. His fourth child Mary was born at this time and perhaps it meant he was at home at Clacton helping care his wife Queenie and the other three youngsters - Paddy, Patricia and John. New members of cast, were compared with the conspicuously absent Phyllis Monkman, Laddie Cliff and Gilbert Childs. Davy Burnaby lifted the show singing about an accountant called "The balloonatics!".

In between munching Terry's chocolates at the interval or leisurely browsing through their programme again at home, it could be seen for theatre buffs that - *The Prisoner of Zenda* by Anthony Hope was on at the Palace. The escape of Rudolph Rassendale might be exciting for younger members of the family or perhaps they would prefer *Treasure Island* at St James. The adventures of David Balfour could be equally exciting. Peg leg Long John Silver craftily stumping about the stage would be fascinating too. The invalid Robert Louis Stevenson's story, written only forty years before was established in theatrical repertoire. The cast enjoyed performing this play, firing the imagination of boys and girls of all ages..

Programmes from various *Co-Optimist* shows, list Stanley's involvement in many ways. 'A pirates dilemma' (could well have been Long John Silverish!). In *Marie Rose Marie,* acceptable ways were found to *send up* the famous Rudolf Friml show about the Mounties.

33

Many folk at home had fun at meal and other times singing to husband or child -
"When I'm calling you ooo ooo", expecting a reply - "Will you answer true ooo ooo!".

Stanley was introduced for a change as - 'The Whispering Baritone'. In
'Spanish Holloway, or write to John Bull about it!", Betty Chester, who had married
Billyard Leak but retained her stage name for obvious reasons, played the part of
Carmencita. Therefore Davy Burnaby was Carmen using the pantomime dame privilege. Not
to be outdone Gilbert Childs was Carmen-two-seater! They all had great fun on a stage
resembling a bull ring, and the audience loved it.

In yet another show, Stanley's sketch and recitation - 'Our Albert' (supported by
Gilbert Childs and Doris Bentley) preceded, and may well have prompted the choice of name
a few years later, of the boy who became lion fodder. In the second half of that show -
'Orpheus, Cupid and Bacchus' was a sketch with Davy Burnaby and Gilbert Childs. Stanley
was the boosey one of the trio. It is easy to imagine them prancing around in togas wearing
laurel leaf crowns!. After 'Lackerlady', the full company joined in a 'Texas Romp' -
Cowboys, Cowgirls and Cow Optimists, brought the Wild West to the theatre.

The B.B.C. helped popularise the *Co-Optimists* by broadcasting excerpts from shows.
Peter Eckersley began his career with B.B.C. as a *disc jockey* as the job is now called.
He introduced gramophone recordings on the air sometimes featuring Stanley's fine singing
voice. This type of entertainment has been popular and significantly used ever since.
On one occasion in the studio at Savoy Hill, Stanley sang and then left the microphone.
The next item was from a young cellist and *John Barbirolli* played!

Stanley avidly followed the cricket scores of county players and England's Test
Matches. He opened his newspaper one summer day and noticed the tennis players -

Monsieurs Lacoste and Cochet who sent the balls whizzing backwards and forward best over the net at Wimbledon, took turns to wrest the challenge trophy for the men's open championship in the famous grass court tournaments. Did Stanley favour the light or dark blues to win the Thames Varsity Boat Race over four gruelling miles from Putney to Mortlake? Oxford were not yet prepared to relinquish their hold on a long unbeaten run of victories. Such topics were discussed by Stanley at the theatre with cast and stage crew relaxing between scenes.

Politicians were beginning to appreciate the importance of radio in communication. Information was conveyed quickly and clearly into many homes in the land. The 'British Broadcasting *Company* was formed in 1927. An announcement said the United Kingdom had gone on the international gold monetary standard. News was very pleasing about a small quantity of gold coming back to England in the form of medals. Harold Abrahams in 100 metres, Scot, Eric Liddell - 400 metres and Douglas Lowe in the 800 metres races, excelled themselves at the Olympic Games in Paris. This thrilling news flashed around the world! The dashing athletic trio surprised their opponents and everyone with their prowess.

On stage Stanley enjoyed quality performances of others. He liked Billy Williams singing "Oh I must go home tonight". Billy Bennett was a comedian Stanley admired. Name dropping was as significant then as it is now. Stanley remembered *Co-Ops* producer Archie de Bear illustrating this point. Archie fancied himself a bit as a songwriter. The ideas he offered Melville Gideon were considered unworthy of consideration. Archie said he had met a chap named Bennett on the Isle of Wight. No, not the one who had roared around the Isle of Man and won the Tourist Trophy race recently on his motor bike, or the comedian they all knew. It was Arnold Bennett who suggested some lines for a funny song. Melville showed

35

some interest and Archie said it went like this:-   "The wild men of Borneo

they never wear a hat, their locks are never shorn-eo not worn-eo like that!"

Melville Gideon was so impressed, believing the author wrote it that he set the words to

music. The *Co-Ops* included the song in their show. After some months Archie told Stanley

he had never ever met Arnold Bennett! At least the lyric was accepted and proved useful!

During interviews when he had finally retired, Stanley recounted various experiences. He

told how the show had to be packed up and moved from Margate to Harrogate. It was typical

that after the last performance on a Saturday night, hopefully to a fuller house, the stage had

to be vacated as quickly as possible. The company then travelled and snatched brief rests

whenever they could until they arrived. Almost immediately they would have to set up at the

theatre in the next town. Once they settled into their lodgings or hotel, Laddie Cliff

seemed to take a very long time in the bathroom. When they asked after him he replied

"Oh I'm all right thanks. I've just been writing out a song I turned over in my mind on the

journey." The song was "When the sun goes down" and, when set to music it proved a

useful addition to his repertoire.

Stanley never said anything about the *Co-Op's* trip to Paris for a short season. He did tell a

story about changing of venue which involved the troupe moving from Newcastle to

Bradford with all their gear. They became held up behind some slow traffic. Everyone was a

bit worried about arriving in good time. When eventually they did manage to free

themselves from the traffic jam, as they moved on they saw the cause as they overtook a

convoy of circus vehicles complete with marquees and elephants. Arriving at the Alhambra

theatre, the *Co-Ops* all helped with unloading the scenery, props and costumes. The curtain

did go up on time but the company knew sometimes "life for them was not so funny!".

36

The finale of " Hit the Deck," the new and deservedly successful musical piece at the Hippodrome. Seated in the centre of the picture are Stanley Holloway, Ivy Tresmand, Sydney Howard and Alice Morley, the principals in this bright show.

CHAPTER FIVE

There's no business like show business.

The original Co-Optimist principals were much in demand to star in other shows.

Davy Burnaby, Betty Chester and Laddie Cliff were in a new show "Bow-Wow". The title

had obviously been chosen from the funny refrain in the Co-Ops chorus. Houdini the

escapologist entertained by managing to get out of almost anything. Stanley needed the

chance to get into something. In 1927, as a Matelot, he *Hit the Deck* nightly at the London

Hippodrome. The show was tried out at the Alhambra, Glasgow. Weston and Lee had

revised the script. Stanley was cast as Bill Smith (not Bilge as he was known in U.S.A).

Hit the Deck was a revival of musical play by Vincent Youmans. This musical was based

on the story 'Shore Leave'. The anglicized version of *Hit the Deck*, in which Stanley

appeared, had changed the setting instead from Newport Rhode Island to Plymouth, Devon.

The U.S. Ship Nebraska was now H.M.S. Inscrutable. A critic wrote - "In being a sailor, reluctant to love, Stanley brought to the role a consistency and insight into the character, not usually found in musical comedy." Ivy Tresmand sang the 'Happy' duet with Stanley - "Sometimes I'm happy, sometimes I'm blue". Stanley also sang the solo - "Fancy me just meeting you". Ivy said - "Stanley was a lovely performer and generous partner to work with." In entertainment over the years, artists may accidentally or deliberately adopt elements of another's style, making it uniquely their own. When Stanley later heard the Andrews Sisters on a record, they reminded him of the Pride Sisters in *Hit the Deck.* Stanley said audiences experiencing the American way of stage presentation, took time to adjust to it. People were a bit surprised and rather shocked at the chorus girls making their entry from the back of the stage through the mens' parted legs.

Hit the Deck, PLOT: Loulou Martin, runs a coffee house in Plymouth. To clarify their relationship she travels after Bill, whom she loves, to the other side of the world. The contrasting mysterious eastern setting is a Chinese Mandarin's house.

CAST: Loulou Martin - Ivy Tresmand Bill Smith - Stanley Holloway

 Magnolia - Alice Morley Lt. Clark - Gerald Nodin

 Lottie Payne - Mamie Watson Matt Barlow - Dick Francis

 Donkey - Reg Sheridan Battling Smith - Sydney Howard

Two popular solo and chorus numbers were "Join the navy" and "Sing Hallelujah".
Principal George Bass fell ill in Glasgow production and Sydney Howard replaced him.
The show ran for 227 performances during nine months in London. One young member of the audience, Alan J. Lerner, who was visiting England, met Stanley for the first time.

Stanley said it was a vintage year for him being at the Hippodrome. There were nine musicals and seven thrillers on in London, all of them American. *The Girl Friend* at the

Palace by Rodgers and Hart included a song sung by a character cycling -

"We'll have a new room a blue room where every day's a holiday".

Stanley also saw *The Vagabond King* by Rudolf Friml. The plot of this musical was that a

Frenchman, made king for a day, thwarted a revolution. It included the memorable song

"Only a rose I give you". *Showboat* by Jerome Kern at the Ziegfield Theatre was setting

higher new standards of performance and also took Broadway by storm. Such examples

showed it was a lively formative time for Stanley to be living in. He, the cast and

management were pleased with the deserved success in 1927 of *Hit the Deck*. The public

enjoyed the tunes and it competed well with *The Desert Song* at Drury Lane.

Another musical to watch from America was George and Ira Gershwin's, *O- Kay*.

which was all the rage at His Majesty's in September, 1927. From imported records, *flappers*

were all ready to join in with Gertrude Lawrence and Noel Coward, tapping their feet

singing - "Do, do, do what you done, done, done before baby!".

Stanley was in rehearsal in Liverpool in 1928 for a new show *The Song of the Sea* .

Late one evening Leslie Henson suddenly appeared to see how his protege was getting on.

The two men talked so much that the leading lady, Lilian Davies , told producer Jack Hulbert

she would have to retire to her bed or she would be incapable of singing the next day.

Stanley remarked "It was the first time a leading lady had walked out on him!"

In 1928, on September 6th, in a lavish musical comedy production of *The Song of the Sea*

at His Majesty's theatre, Stanley, was promoted officer, from able seaman scrubbing decks.

The *Song of the Sea* PLOT: a story akin to the romance of Lord Horatio Nelson and Emma

Hamilton. A wench at the Pelican Inn, Portsmouth falls in with the plans of Sir William

THE PLAY

PICTORIAL

"SONG OF THE SEA"

No.
321

Candysshe, and to improve her lot marries him. As Lady Candysshe she helps to free her infuriated lover, Manners, from jail. This rags to riches nautical story, produced by Claud Hulbert is set on the deck of H.M.S. Conquest and at the British Embassy in Naples.

CAST: Nancy, Lady Candysshe - Lilian Davies

Sir Wyllyam Candysshe   -   Dennis Hoey

Lieutenant Richard Manners   Stanley Holloway.

Supporting cast - Mary Leigh, A.W. Baskcomb, Winifred Hare, Polly Ward & Edna Covey. Reports said "Lilian stood, radiantly, in full length white gown, singing the duet "True Eyes" with Stanley Holloway. The mere fact the cast comprises such polished artists as Stanley Holloway ensures the quality of the production".

It was a very important leading role for Stanley to play. "We love you lovely lady" was another ballad. The chorus sang the popular breezy title song. Producer Claude Hulbert also played the part of courier Bob Blake. Some members of the audience saw a resemblance to the plot of Gilbert and Sullivan's *H.M.S. Pinafore*

There were advertisements in the 1928 programme for goods and services. Members of the audience could take a winter cruise to South Africa for only £170 1st or £140 2nd class. Ladies admiring Miss Davies could like her, use Ponds Vanishing cream to improve their complexion. This cosmetic to add to their dressing table cost half a crown (12½p) a jar.

In February 1929, Stanley achieved a goal sought by every entertainer. He was invited to appear at the London Palladium. The show was called *Our Flat* with Isobel Elsom, Billy Merson, Irene Shamrock, Oona Mayer and old Co-Ops pal Wolseley Charles (the cardinal!) supported by Al Lymans band. Stanley thought he just couldn't sing songs in his programme. A word with Leslie Henson came up with a story Roy Royston had told him.

41

It was about a soldier who dropped his musket and wouldn't pick it up. Such disobedience was certainly different. At home alone in his room during a sleepness night, while his wife Queenie nursed the children who all had whooping cough, Stanley jotted down words in pencil on the back of an envelope. In ten minutes he had the gist of a monologue about - "Sam and his musket". The name Small for Sam was based on Leslie Henson's housekeeper Annie Small. Stanley tried out the monologue in between hearty baritone songs like "Come to the cookhouse store". The seed of his unique style of monologues was sown.

By the Spring of 1929 the trend in musical theatre entertainment changed in the direction of vaudeville shows. Stanley teamed up with Claude Hulbert again in *Coo-ee. It was* a two part revue with music by Melville Gideon staged at the Vaudeville theatre. A critic noted "Dorothy Dickson danced well and was the *bluebird* to whom Stanley sang - "Balcony Girl". The sketch was reminiscent of entertainment at the Music Hall when Stanley was growing up. From up in the gallery, Stanley had waved his handkerchief at Nellie Power or Marie Lloyd. In the second half of *Coo-ee*, Stanley was Mrs. Posney dressed in drag, Billy Bennett was Mrs Codrington and Claude Hulbert played Mrs. Darling. The sketch was called 'Work Tea'. In another piece Stanley played Othello and if parody can be counted, this was his very first small taste of Shakespeare.

Coo-ee! ran for only two months. A critic said "Billy Bennett was a star who did not include subtlety in his make up. Stanley Holloway is one of the funniest versatile artists on the musical stage. He was excellent throughout, especially so in "She's funny that way" and "Sam, Sam, pick up tha' musket". It is a bright amusing revue and the audience liked it immensely." The rest of the cast were Dorothy Dickson, Wyn Richmond, Charles Collins, Josie Melville, Joan Clarkson with De Haven and Nice. However when The Times reviewed

42

the show they it was said very poor. "Two droll ballet dancers, not named in the programme, were the best of a very disappointing evening." Perhaps the reporter should have taken a tip from another programme and been watching Somerset Maugham's - 'The Sacred Flame' at the Playhouse. Gladys Cooper and Sebastian Shaw had the leading roles for patrons of more serious theatre. In 1929 more attention was being paid in England to film making. The early work of Friese-Green and others had been developed until probably the first sound musical was made here. Stanley and the Co-Optimists stars were brought together for the purpose. It was experimental and Stanley was surprised the producer just filmed their acts. The title leant itself to a full story behind the scenes showing how they were founded.

The daily newspapers Stanley read told of telephone boxes being built in many streets. Three people in every 100 now rented a telephone. Half a million people over the age of 65 received the first State Pensions. Stanley wasn't quite ready for his yet! The popular Noel Coward song of the time was - "A room with a view". It came from his show *This Year of Grace*. Frequently broadcast, it appealed to some people's romantic needs. Short wave radio reached the whole of the empire.

An unusual opportunity occurred for Stanley to record with the B.B.C. -

'Alice's Adventures in Wonderland and Through the Looking Glass'.

A star CAST of distinctive voices was chosen including:- Joan Greenwood as Alice, Florence Desmond as the Duchess, Richard Goolden - caterpillar, Robertson Hare - gryphon, Ronald Frankau - Humpty Dumpty, Sydney Walker - Cheshire Cat and Arthur Askey as the Mad Hatter.

Stanley Holloway was Tweedle Dee to his old friend Leslie Henson's Tweedle Dum.

43

Tweedle Dum and Tweedle Dee

In the autumn of 1929, the Co-Optimists revived their show, at the Vaudeville Theatre in the Strand. Topical items included a sketch - 'Hammersmith Broadway melody' In this the was attacked as it was seriously affecting live theatre audiences.

The talkies had arrived in 1927 with Al Jolson in 'The Jazz Singer'. His "You ain't heard nothin yet" had decimated former queues at theatre box offices. In the show Stanley introduced a song called "Beware". It was about a green eyed monster dragon with 13 tails. About the revised *Co-Optimists* show, one critic commented "Not all the songs were as good as this one - about the melodically sinuous "Green Dragon" which Mr. Holloway sings with such point and spirit." Incidentally, the Dragon's menu included Policeman pie and roast M.P. for dinner! Other turns varied in the *Co-Optimists* new show were Phyllis Monkman skilfully illustrating Ella Shields singing "Burlington Bertie from Bow". When this song first came out, it had been the key to women attending the crude unsavoury male world of Music Hall. They daringly dressed as men, drag costume enabling them appear on stage, just as earlier some women found it useful to be in male audiences.

Billy Mayerl was writing and playing a lot of music for the troupe. Stanley, with light

44

step and smile, cheerfully sang "Tommy the whistler" and a contrasting negro spiritual imitating Paul Robeson. The parts in 'The Four Horsemen of the Apocalypse' showing the revelation of an even newer era, were played by:- Laddie Cliff (Mirth), Gilbert Childs (Misery) Davy Burnaby (Famine) and Stanley Holloway's (Orgy)!

The *Original Co-Ops* toured the provinces.

Phyllis Monkman did a song and dance routine

with Stanley - 'The Clean Up' -

direct from the Ziegfield follies.'

Stanley dressed as a farm yokel sang -

"I'm leaning on the gate beside the pond."

Old sheets of music commemorate solos by

talented Co-Optimists.

- "I'm Ticked to death I'm single".

Laddie also made a big hit singing his -

"Coal Black Mammy" like G.H. Elliott.

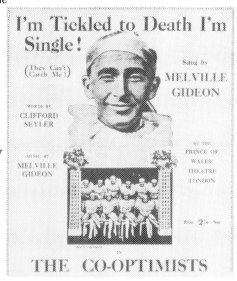

A Theatre magazine correspondent wrote, after seeing a performance one very warm evening

"In the heat, the show required physical and moral courage. So indefegatible are

the Co-Optimists that the spirit of the audience quickens to meet theirs,   lessening the

labour until it becomes a co-operative business. In other words they grin and bear it!"

Another newspaper cutting of 1929 said "At our instigation, they find themselves

perpetual *Vicars of Bray* and he must be a donkey who would not rejoice in the rendition of

jocund manifestation!" The reporter seems to choose a flowery language reminiscent of

masters of ceremonies at music halls.

A sketch 'One Lung Two' seemed again to feed on the eastern tradition in theatre established by Chu Chin Chow. Perhaps too, it prepared Stanley for eastern garments when he later appeared in pantomime. In this he sang a duet with Elsa Macfarlane "Wonderful Day", before being a policeman in an amusing routine - 'Never get excited'. Stanley's versatility and success in portraying a wide range of parts fuelled his career. As Philip de Smythe said in 'Wordy Warfare' - Stanley showed off his ability to act characters. Next he appeared in 'My Ladies Eyes'. The scenario was partly at the clubhouse and partly in Mrs. Gordon's boudoir. Naturally not all criticisms were favourable. A scathing piece appeared in one newspaper. "What is really the matter with the present revival is that, these admirable artists seem to expect that a number of items of no particular entertainment, amount, when added up to a sum of delight. If they were satisfied I wasn't!"

When the Co-Ops returned to Birmingham it was very frankly reported that - "The Co-Optimists came unstuck, stymied by old blue boar ballad of unimpeachable banality. The performance was fragrant with the dust of ages!". Was it the Press who stung them? The Co-Optimists company reacted ? A review in the Telegraph in 1930 thought they did.They recognised - "Bright fun in new show. Old guard and new recruits offer witty parodies. After initial greetings, there was Mr. Burnaby as a guard on a Channel tunnel train. A Jules Verne effort!" (remarkably predicting the future 60 years on when Le Shuttle materialised.) "After a jolly song composed by Wolseley Charles," the reporter continued, "Stanley Holloway - exercises more generously than of old, the admirable gift of parodying his contemporaries. This is enhanced by his fine baritone voice".

In July 1930, in the successful or disastrous real world outside the theatre, news came that the commercial airship R100 had flown safely to Canada and back. The youth Nevil

Norway, whom lieutenant Holloway had seen helping with First Aid rescue in Dublin, was

the chief calculator for Vickers. Norway was obliged to travel on the maiden voyage whereas

designer, Barnes Wallis, wasn't. Stuttering Nevil, flying high over the St.Lawrence river in

the R 100, actually, bravely held some torn canvas together until Captain Meager repaired it.

The world was shaken on 5th October, when the government financed airship R 101

crashed at Beauvais. Lord Thompson Minister of Aviation had desperately needed to

open up an air route to India for the prestige of the British Empire.

After not fully testing alterations and noting weather forecast, the impatient Thompson set

off in the R 101. Was his excess baggage another factor in causing the disaster?

Nevil Norway, whom Stanley had seen in Dublin in other troublesome times, was sorry at

not being transferred to work on that project. His life though was saved and, after founding

Airspeed Aircraft in York, he started writing novels using his christian names -

NEVIL SHUTE. His first book 'So Distained', could be bought in 1928. He used the

fictional idea of photographic reconnaissance over Portsmouth, from flying over it himself.

Stanley was glad of his own photographic memory for it helped him to remember

over 100 pages of 40 rhyming story monologues. Forgetfulness in front of an audience can

be very embarrassing. A new broadcaster was Sandy Powell, a north country comedian.

He dropped his script in the studio whilst on the air and went on talking in front of the *mike*.

Listeners heard "Can you hear me mother?". The catch phrase stayed with him for the

whole of his career. Stanley too admitted once *drying up* during reciting a monologue in front

of an audience. He quickly asked them - "I bet you can't tell me what the next line is?". They

could and did enabling him to finish the monologue!.

The successful revival of the Co-Optimists show in 1930 listed many sketches in which

47

Stanley Holloway was involved as - Simple Simon Q.C. in 'The Divorce of the Painted Doll', 'Operatic Househunting', 'A Dotty Drama' with Herbert Munden and a duet with Sylvia Cecil 'I'm satisfied'. The whole company were on stage for 'Family Album'. Other titles were - 'Love Lies Bleeding - a co-pessimists lament!' and 'Bertie Brown' was a romp enacted with interruptions. Stanley was the stranger in 'Stowman the mow' a variation on the well known round for singing - "One man went to mow, went to mow a meadow".

There had been another almost complete turnover in cast of the *Co-Optimists*. Only Phyllis Monkman, Elsa Macfarlane, Davy Burnaby and Stanley Holloway remained the nucleus of founder members. New names, some promoted from the Co-Optimists touring company that visited the Sparrows Nest Theatre at Lowestoft in Suffolk were:- Joan Barrie, Mimi Crawford, Eric le Fray, Elsie Randolph, Stewart Ross, and Joe Sergeant. Herbert Munden was transferred to the first team and was a waiter at table while Stanley sang with Elsa Macfarlane.

The news media suggested there were internal squabbles among older members of the Co-Ops. Wolseley Charles had replaced pianist Harry S. Pepper who went to the B.B.C. Once established at Broadcasting House, Harry revived a White Coon show, (he too was - *Following* in father's footsteps) and Stanley was happy to appear and help him.

On 27th April, 1931, *The Original Co-Optimists* appeared at the New Theatre, Cambridge. To open with a number "Cheerio Pierrot" seemed to forecast the impending end of tradition. Davy Burnaby was in "The Old Guard - supported by the star company including Martell and Henessey!" (Maybe no financial sponsorship was donated by the best names in brandy?). In the second half Billy Mayerl played 'My Turkish Delight - oriental splendour, proving the yeast rises even higher than the vest!" The whole company took part

48

in the satire on 'Jack and Jill - a *pail* phantom of a nursery rhyme!' in which Stanley sang a

duet with Phyllis Monkman - "The house that Jack built." An item 'The Co-Optimist

punishment - Spring Punions' was followed also by the whole company as a 'Band of Hope

and Glory' singing "Schultz is back again". The last performance closed to mark the end of

an era of unsophisticated shows.

Over seven years, The Co-Optimists had done 1,568 shows taking over £300,000 at the

door. Theatres in the provinces in winter were packed at Brighton (1925), Newcastle (1926)

and Torquay (1927). People enjoyed this kind of touring concert party. After the month of

August off on holiday, the team met up again and a new programme was prepared. Leslie

Henson told The Stage magazine reporter for a regrets article - "My biggest disappointment

was not investing £100 in 1921 when invited to support *Co-Optimists*. It would have repaid

more than £4,000!"

Stanley attributed the somewhat surprising success to the combination of talents. "If

you had a million pounds in 1970 and you were asked to put on another *Co-Optimists* show

you probably couldn't do it. You couldn't buy it, you see. It was just one of those things that

happened." In the early years here was hardly any animosity among the members.

Apparently, according to David Stucky of Card Times, Stanley was registered as bankrupt

following the end of Co-Optimists shows. Stanley was an employee and not a share holder.

This was at the time of the international monetary slump. Yet he went to U.S.A.

In 1933 Stanley made his first visit to America with Jack and Claude Hulbert and renewed

meeting Alan Lerner. The news from Europe was of the Reichstag fire in Germany.

In April 1934 at Drury Lane, Stanley appeared in *The Three Sisters*.

He was police constable Eustace Titherley. Jerome Kern and Oscar Hammerstein were here

49

from America to produce and conduct the musical show. The scenes are at Epsom racecourse on Derby Day and at the front in wartime.

Esmond Knight played a significant part as a gypsy.

Well known artist, Dorothy Dickson was also in the cast. Stanley, as a jealous policeman thought one reason for the failure of the show *The Three Sisters* was that talented Dorothy Dickson, a public idol, had such a small part to play.

The public showed their disapproval by giving *the bird* in the traditional Music Hall manner!

Although the show was not very successful, one of the good tunes -"I won't dance" survived. It was salvaged later for use in another show *Roberta*. The Three Sisters had at least given Stanley the experience of working for the first time at the Theatre Royal. He learned of something of American stage production methods. During the show Stanley also worked in a film on Sundays. He travelled up to Blackpool to take a small part as a policeman in a film Gracie Fields was making - *'Sing as we Go'*. Stanley found filming very interesting. His chats off the set with Gracie Fields influenced his career She knew what he did on stage and told him, with his capabilities, he should do more variety solo work.

As a choirboy, in his grass roots days, Stanley had quite enjoyed sacred music like

"The Dream of Gerontius". In 1934 the composer Sir Edward Elgar died. The B.B.C.

national newscasters reported with *pomp and circumstance*, attendance at the funeral of the

*enigma*tical Worcestershire musician. More worrying news for everyone was about

Germany re-arming. Winston Churchill was reported as saying - "We have never been so

defenceless as we are now". Most people were disinterested, too busy improving their lives

after the slump. "Anything Goes" was the attitude, expressed in a Cole Porter song from

New York. House purchasers though could then buy new homes for £400 cash or 10/- (50p)

per month for life. A site of a great exhibition was being prepared at the Crystal Palace.

CHAPTER SIX

First monologues , recordings and films.

As a youth Stanley saw monologues at the music hall. Charles Russell did one at the

turn of the century called 'Patriotism'. When his *number came up* Russell entered from the

wings on to the dimly lit stage, wearing tropical costume with a solar tope hat, as they did in

the colonies. A man dressed as a native, already lay cowering on the floor. Two men who

resembled arabs were just about to take this prisoner to slavery. Russell stood with his foot

on the prone slave. Pointing a pistol at each of the heads of the would be captors he recited

some moving words of freedom, commending the advantages of being in the British Empire.

One day in Shaftesbury Avenue, during the *Co-Optimist's* run, Stanley met Walter Midgely. Walter had been music director at the Empire theatre, Hartlepool in 1919, when Stanley was demobilised there. On hearing that Ernest Hastings had died, Stanley added the monologues to his repertoire. Stanley remembered seeing Hastings, wearing pince-nez, recite them. One was - "And yet I Don't know" - how to deal with the problem of choosing a wedding present. The other - "My word you do look queer" was about a sick man who is cruelly treated and nearly driven to death by critical acquaintances until a friend encourages and puts new life into him.

Marriott Edgar, known as George, was the stepson of thriller author Edgar Wallace. A Scotsman, George's first experience in entertainment was at the Grand Theatre Islington on 16th August 1897. He appeared at the Empire in Leicester Square in 1904. He took part in pantomimes, helped paint scenery and joined the famous concert party the Fol-de-Rols. Like Stanley he was steeped in theatrical life. He wrote sketches for concert party, revue and pantomime. He went on to write screen plays for films starring Will Hay.

Marriott Edgar wrote a humorous dramatic recitation about Joe Lee, the channel swimmer who loses the support tugboat in the fog. It was a topical idea and well received. The New Yorker, Gertrude Ederle, had swum the English Channel in 1926, in 14 hours 31 minutes. Miss Ederle's courageous effort of endurance interested the public. Other strong swimmers trained hard to make attempts to beat her record.

Marriott Edgar then concentrated his creative thoughts on a new idea for a monologue in Lancashire dialect, based on the news that a boy had been mauled and eaten by a lion at the zoo. Albert Ramsbottom was to be the unfortunate boy and Wallace seemed a natural enough choice for the name of the Lion. Little did Edgar know it would give him some immortality but in a very different way from the pen of his famous relation. Marriott Edgar handed the written draft of 'Albert' to Stanley Holloway whilst he was in the wings at a theatre. Stanley just slipped it in his pocket.

Sam Small had arisen from adapting a hearsay comment from Leslie Henson. The story proved to be - 'The King and the Volunteer' from Evelyn Waugh's 'Cronies at an Inn'. The same idea with different rhyming words reached and amused a far larger public. Skilled adaptation of material was becoming an even more important part of theatrical life. As far back as 1910, George Bernard Shaw had reluctantly agreed to have his play - *'Arms and the Man'* made into a musical show. *The Chocolate Soldier* by Oscar Strauss went on at the Lyric Theatre in London having done well in Vienna and New York. It began the integration of the European operetta tradition into American musical shows. Stanley and everyone enjoyed singing the latest hit - "My Hero", "Come, come, I love you only my heart is true".

Written talent may be expressed in many various ways. Copying, if too obvious is frowned upon and is not very commendable. The writer of the book Ecclesiastes points out - "There is nothing new under the sun". The widow of a captain of a First World War submarine sent Stanley a plaque with words from Ecclesiastes engraved upon it. The wise words from chapter 9, verses 11 to 18 hung on his bedroom wall:-
"The race is not to the swift nor the battle to the strong but time and chance happeneth to them all. The words of wise men are heard in quiet. Wisdom is better than war."

Stanley's interest in cricket for relaxation was spurred on with the rest of the fans at the news - "Percy Fender scores 100 runs in 35 minutes! The fastest century so far." *Call Boy* won the Derby and Joe Davis commanded the world at snooker. Stanley's challenge was in a different den of sport. He went back up north to entertain in cabaret.

He had been asked as a guest, to entertain at a Northern Rugby League club dinner in 1929 at Newcastle. He wondered what to do and he had read over the Albert and the Lion monologue when he found the paper in his pocket after a show. It seemed a good chance to try it out on a critical audience.

Everyone was busy eating, drinking, and talking about the rugby season. For Stanley it was like the music hall. Entertainers had to attract attention. The chairman banged the table. Stanley stood on a chair:-

"There's a famous seaside place called Blackpool that's noted for fresh air and fun and Mr and Mrs. Ramsbottom went there with young Albert, their son."

Ramsbottom

The clinking of cutlery and glasses did not completely stop but he spoke up and went on. When he got to the moment of the reaction of the lion, Wallace, to having a stick pushed into his ear, intrigued laughter began. Munching, chat and drinking had stopped. After the last line about *"feeding ruddy lions"*, everyone clapped and showed they had been very amused by the yarn. Stanley said later - "After that it was a sure fire monologue for me".

Stanley tried his hand at song writing. With pianist Leo Cornish in the style of "My Old Dutch" he wrote an original song about "Mrs. Brahn who's known as Mrs. B.". He held the copyright and although not a very best seller there was some demand for it.

Stanley was becoming well known. 'Old Sam' picking up his musket was a public figure questioning authority. Many people at home learned to recite:-

"It occurred on the evening before Waterloo and troops were lined up on parade

The sergeant inspecting 'em he was a terror of whom every man was afraid".

Stanley wrote a sequel "'Alt! Who goes there?". Palace sentry Sam can't believe the person

answering his challenge is King George the Fourth because he hadn't a crown on. Wearing a

bowler hat in the rain the king asks him in for a cup of tea. Listeners loved the outrageously

human natural portrayal of royalty.

Gilbert and Sullivan had introduced references to royalty, which might have been

thought disrespectful in Queen Victoria's time. The heirs apparent to be King of Barataria

relate:- "rising early in the morning we proceed to light the fire!". The Queen showed her

approval by surprisingly asking Sir Arthur Sullivan particularly for *The Gondoliers* to be

performed at Windsor on March 6th, 1891 and not one of his more serious works.

Bob Weston and Bert Lee were quite well known in the theatrical profession as *plumbers*.

This meant they could take an American show like *Hit the deck*, in which Stanley appeared

and reset the words, story and songs to suit English audiences. Bob Weston was completely

deaf but he was a very competent composer. In spite of this disability, his skills in light

music were of course far more modest compared to Beethoven's but he had a contribution to

make to entertainment. Weston and Lee had written several hit songs suited to the styles of

particular artists. "Goodbyee" was sung by Harry Tate. "I'm 'Enery the eighth I am"

is associated with Harry Champion and "Heaven will protect an honest girl"- Gracie Fields.

Weston and Lee had also written, ten years previously, the two monologues for Ernest

Hastings. Many artists had clever chat and patter songs in their turns but the monologue was

rather a special genre and Stanley was just the right exponent of it. In 1931, Weston and Lee

55

wrote 'Beat the retreat on thy drum'. Rather like a limerick writing craze, lots of people now tried their hands at writing monologues. Some subjects became a vogue as a more entertaining way for children to learn history.

The 1920' was proving to be a livelier time as people slowly emerged from Victorian restraints. There was a bit more freedom to experiment for those who cared and dared to do so. The wax cylindrical recording drums of Edison Bell on Gem players had been further improved by flat discs. Business boomed on phonographs or gramophones which played the catchy styles of new music mostly from America.

Stanley and individual or ensemble members of the Co-Optimists were frequently needed at the recording studios. Some of the difficulties of performing into a large funnel had been overcome and more clear accurate recordings were being achieved. Income Tax stamps for a farthing had to be paid. 'Magic Notes' was the Columbia trade mark. Stanley made a record of Albert and the Lion.

Commission from the Columbia Company based in London E.C.1, supplemented his income. Over a million were sold. For H.M.V. in November 1922 on label B-1441, Stanley recorded "The Wild Man of Borneo". Melville Gideon accompanied the number he had been tricked into writing.

The H.M.V. trade mark was a little dog patiently sitting on the polished top of his master's coffin. The dog has looked quizzically down the output horn for over a century. In music shop windows the boom was seen in attractive displays, of records. This included lion motif of Rex, the Crystalate Gramophone Record Company. Their factory was in the East End at 60, City Road, London E.C.1. 'The Eagle' public house was near their premises. This pub was mentioned in the music hall song by W. Mandale:-

"Half a pound of tuppeny rice, ½ a pound of treacle.

That's the way the money goes 'pop' goes the weasel

Up and down the City Road in and out of 'The Eagle'

That's the way the money goes, pop goes the weasel". (getting money from a pawnbroker)

Other manufacturers were Fox and Winner with obvious eye catching illustrations on their record sleeves. Broadcast, Zonophone, Parlophone records were competing with prestigious sounding names like- Imperial, Embassy and Regal. Some of the finest examples of Stanley's singing are:- "Sometimes I'm Happy" from *Hit the Deck*, "It'll be all the same a 100 years from now" from *A Night Out*, "Onaway Awake beloved" from Hiawatha wedding and from - *The Three Sisters*, a lovely ballad - "Hand in hand we'll walk together".

The whole range of music from brass bands to ballet was made available in their homes to anyone who wanted and could afford it. At 78 revolutions per minute, the 10 or 12 inch discs went round on the turntable and a steel needle picked up and reproduced the sound from the grooves. As the clockwork spring ran down, some hasty rewinding was necessary to avoid peculiar increasingly slurred sounds and words.

In the early days some artists refused to be recorded. Their philosophy was that people listening to records at home would not pay to visit theatres to see artists. While there was

57

some wisdom in their reticence, a share of the profits from record sales was a big incentive to

be recorded. Therefore artists increasingly agreed to make recordings. Today, television

presents a similar problem, in that new material of live performers is seen or heard briefly

once and millions of people know it. An artist has to work all the year round.

A rare durium recorded disc was made in 1931 at the invitation of Ramsay Macdonald's

government during a financial crisis. We don't know if having Sam Small at Westminster

helped in any early way to sort out a balance of the economy. (Nat. Govt. film 2692)

To relax from working in the heat and smell of theatres or cramped recording studios,

Stanley took an occasional break in the fresher air. He watched cricket being played at

Kennington Oval or Lord's, the headquarters of Marylebone Cricket Club (M.C.C.) at St.

John's Wood. Stanley became a non playing member. The matches attracted many thousands

of spectators to grounds to see heroes Sutcliffe and Rhodes. In white flannels they batted

bravely in the hot sunshine jousting against the dangerous fast deliveries of Larwood.

One compensation for his trying work was that Stanley travelled around the country. On

tour in the Midlands in summer, his visit might coincide with a chance to see some cricket.

Edgbaston, Birmingham; Trent Bridge, Nottingham; or Old Trafford, Manchester.

Scenes of famous test matches at these grounds and at and Headingly, Leeds, sometimes

conveniently occurred when Stanley was performing at a nearby city theatre.

In July 1930 the Australian Donald Bradman scored a phenomenal record 344 runs. English

legendary batsmen Frank Woolley and Patsy Hendren did their best. Hope for regaining the

Ashes was raised by fast bowler Harold Larwood of Nottinghamshire. He was sent with the

England team the infamous *Bodyline* tour of Australia.

The effects of the financial recession and the collapse of the Stock Market on Wall Street in America, troubled everyone's income and spending power, especially entertainers. The short revival of the Co-Optimists and a little income from recordings brought Stanley some relief. Business began to pick up and in 1932, a comedy show, the *Savoy Follies*, went on tour. After being tried out for a week in June at Brighton and Birmingham, the show ran for the month of September at the Savoy Theatre, London. Stanley was in a sketch with Florence Desmond for the Follies. He played the part of a policemen and delayed moving on two tramps (Hal Bryan and John Mack), from a park bench, while they all listened to Florence's money problems. In the second half of the revue by Archie de Bear, Stanley wore a dress suit with a mock Order of the Garter. Hal Swain and his band provided the music. Gillie Potter (with his eccentric speech) Bertha Recardo, Iris Ashley, Polly Ward, Rita Mackay, William Walker and Bobby Alderson made up the group. Teddy Fox, the obese xylophone player was a twinkling star with his quick hammer playing. The chorus sang - "Three little maids from school". They borrowed Japanese costume ideas from the *Mikado* and somehow avoided wrathful copyright proceedings by Bridget D'Oyly Carte. A reporter for the Birmingham Post wrote - "Stanley Holloway has a new song called 'Albert and the Lion' which is as funny as 'Beat the Retreat'. He can parody a Negro spiritual with tasteful lively humour. He can sing an old sentimental ballad either seriously or mock seriously". Keeping the *pot boiling* for the audience they had attracted, *Here we are again* went on at the Lyceum in October, 1932. The Times reporter said "It was a similar to the Savoy Follies. The show was enlivened by two men whose signature tune was - 'He sings the low notes I don't know how he gets 'um, yours very sincerely - Flotsam and Jetsum!' In this show, the comedians Nat Mills and Bobby Jackson supported Gillie Potter ("Good evening England") and the Hal Swain band played again. Mr. Stanley Holloway tells once more the sad story of Our Albert whose father took him to the zoo".

Stanley broadcast monologues regularly on B.B.C. radio. Listeners were invited to send in entries for a competition which he agreed to judge. He said it wasn't easy to choose the best because, interesting as parts of many of them were, they mostly lacked a really good punch line. His stage producer Archie de Bear even wrote one for Stanley in 1933. 'Many Happy Returns' was about the birthday of a Runcorn Headmaster and how the schoolboys dealt with it. Cecil Madden, the B.B.C. producer wrote "Holloway has a grand voice and is an extremely amenable and pleasant fellow to work with". A series of programmes was set up to recite the whole of the growing Sam and Albert collection, written mostly by Marriott Edgar. One wet Saturday morning, Stanley consulted M. Edgar, performing in the Fol-de-Rols season at Hastings, about 'Marksman Sam' whose lack of prowess with the musket earned him five days C.B. - 'Confined to barracks'.

Commercial work was occasionally commissioned. For the Austin Motor Company of Longbridge, Birmingham, Stanley recorded 'Sam's Fortune'. In it Sam Small inherits £150 which he says he is going to invest and not be tempted by extravagant ideas of friends. In the end he invests it in an Austin car - "I'm proud of me judgement" says Sam.
The car " Goes faster than yon blushing greyhound, looks better than films stars on set and as to the pleasure of travel its equal I've not seen yet - developing 25 horse power not only looks good but got guts, it does forty miles to the gallon, got plenty of room and good lines - if police stop us between here and Blackpool I've got ten bob left over for fines!" (p.173)

Stanley obtained some royalties from having his name on the cover of sheets of music. Other welcome income was from appearing on advertisement for cigarettes and tobacco. On Wills Radio Celebrity cigarette cards it described Stanley as - "One of the few first class actors with an excellent singing voice". De Reske portrayed him on a poster smoking their brand. Sets of cigarette cards on many subjects including entertainers, might influence the choice smokers made. The quality and style of advert pictures was not very flattering. Stanley seen here wearing glasses, offers an open cigarette case: Another showing him smoking a pipe, said - "The ten minute smoke for intelligent folk. On A.B.C. chewing -gum cards he doesn't wear glasses.

Many famous people have found a way to make their mark in life in very different ways. The words of Ecclesiastes on the plaque Stanley was given constantly reminded him -there is a time and place for everything.

There are many superstitions backstage in theatres. Whistling is frowned upon and to mention Macbeth is considered unlucky. In the theatre , as stage performers go on, they often say what is meant to be cheerful encouraging advice to overcome nerves - "Good luck - break a leg!". George Robey, with whom Stanley had appeared on stage and in films, literally did once damage a leg, falling off the edge of the stage. He hobbled back on to finish the show. A different performer before crowds, on the race track scene - Gordon Richards, was champion jockey again. He still just loved racing on horses, even though he too twice had to recover from having legs broken in falls from riding.

Stanley's agent, Lilian Asa, represented many famous people in show business from her office in Finchley Road. Agents were always on the look out for vacancies and ways to introduce their clients to new contracts. Artist and agent want ongoing opportunities to perform. The name must be publicised and kept in the eye of the public and producers. On Gracie Fields' advice, Stanley went into pantomime. It was another medium for his talents. He played the part of Abanazar in *Aladdin* at the Prince of Wales Theatre, Birmingham, in 1934. It ran very successfully for three months. His former Co-Optimist colleague Davy Burnaby played Widow Twanky. Ageing Sir Henry Lytton was no stranger to the theatre in Birmingham either. He led many D'Oyly Carte Gilbert and Sullivan productions. From the roles of Sir Joseph Porter in H.M.S. Pinafore, Lord Chancellor in Iolanthe and menial Ko-Ko in the Mikado. He was promoted - Emperor of China. However, many people thought he was past his best as an actor by this time .

A critic wrote about Stanley's role as Abanazar- "Mr Holloway at his first entrance is an Anatolian vagabond. He plays the magician with the most satisfying confidence and ease. He is an artist as well as an artiste, with the attribute of never forcing the situation for effect." " He would not be forgiven" the critic went on " if he did not endow the part with some semblance of the many droll characters created in recent years. There was a roar of delighted applause when he assumed the personality of Mr. Ramsbottom. He told us the sequel to Albert's adventures with the lion".

Impresario Emile Littler was growing in reputation. At the theatre, advertisements in the programme showed that houses could be bought in Birmingham for £475 freehold or £600 leasehold. To raise funds for the Boys and Girls Union in Birmingham, on December 13th at a Christmas market, Stanley autographed copies of his records.

News of the very successful pantomime reached other cities around the country and further bookings were made. On four consecutive winter seasons at Leeds (1935), Golder's Green Hippodrome, London (1936), Edinburgh (1937) and Manchester (1938), Stanley impressed as 'Abanazar' in Aladdin. It was another *string to his bow* in entertainment.

Stanley had been asked by Robert Atkins to appear for him in Shakespeare at Regent's Park Open Air Theatre. Stanley politely refused on advice that he had no experience of the Bard's work and might let himself down. Nevertheless, Stanley knew that sooner or later he would have to come to grips with it.

A show *Life begins at Oxford Circus* was running at the Palladium. Flanagan and Allen were in it and Jack Hylton's band played. Stanley was invited to join in on 8th April 1935. Flanagan and Allen topped the bill. Holland and Hunt, the Four Casting Pearls and Pope and Louie were with Stanley in the supporting cast. Stanley was told he would have to speak some Shakespeare. He felt he would probably teased unmercifully by his comedian friends.

For some advice on Shakespeare, Stanley phoned his old friend Godfrey Tearle. Since their days in the trenches, Godfrey too was getting on well in theatre and films. He had just appeared in 'The Thirty Nine Steps' with Robert Donat and Madeleine Carrol. The film, in black and white, was a popular thriller with cinema audiences. The director Alfred Hitchcock surprised their senses and made a dramatic impact on cinema goers. Godfrey told Stanley, over the phone, the lines of the full Shakespeare speech he needed and where to find it. - "This earth this realm this England" - John of Gaunt, Richard II Act II.

Touring shows offered audiences entertainment at smaller provincial theatres. A company was sometimes hurriedly assembled. Agents like Stanley's Lilian Aza had a good range of artists on their books. In May 1935 Stanley was signed up to appear at the Palace

Blackpool. A motley cast of troubadors included Conrad's Pigeons, El Ray and Lady Duval,

Seven Austrian Tokays, Lilian Gunns, Eugene with his Magyar band and Blanche Collins.

topped the bill at the Birmingham Hippodrome in July and his wife Queenie met him there.

When Stanley sang his monologue "With her 'ead tucked underneath her arm" he tactfully

had the audience sing "She walks, the Blackpool Tower" instead of *'bloody'* as written.

Stanley was invited to appear on the popular B.B.C. radio show Henry Hall's Guest Night

which broadcast from Blackpool. A monologue in north country accent was a simple and

popular choice of contribution. Another broadcast at that time was 'In Town Tonight'. After

the opening signature tune, "Knightsbridge" from Eric Coates "London suite", the sound

effects of the roar of traffic were suddenly and dramatically halted by the word "Stop!".

Listeners at home gained some personal insights into the experiences of famous people

interviewed in the capital.

Stanley was learning to play golf and it was interesting to hear Henry Cotton interviewed,

about winning the Open Golf championship for Britain at last. Another radio guest,

tennis player Peggy Scriven, who had been dropped from the English Women's Davis Cup

team because her of awkward style, explained how she was spurred on to go to Paris and

win the French Open tournament!

Ex army officers like Stanley who had partially idolised Lawrence were shocked by the

B.B.C. announcement his accidental death, on a motorbike in Dorset. In memory

of Lawrence of Arabia, several very high ranking officers attended a quiet funeral at St.

Paul's cathedral, to pay their last respects to a modern cavalier. T.E. Lawrence received

some open recognition and praise for his amazing exploits (on behalf of the interests of the

British and King Faisal) during the Arab/Turkish revolt in Egypt and Palestine.

On the 29th October, 1935, at the London Palladium, Stanley found himself in talented theatrical company for the Royal Variety Show. There were only really two Royal *Command* performances in 1912, from which Marie Lloyd was omitted, and another in 1919. For this occasion Stanley was compere of a 'Cavalcade of Variety' with famous retired artists.

All Wave was another Archie de Bear revue at the Duke of York's Theatre. Naughton Wayne, Peggy Cochrane, Horace Kenny, Jeannie Dean entertained with Stanley. It parodied radio theme sketches and was directly or indirectly set in a broadcasting studio. The Times critic wrote - "Stanley Holloway was too skilled performer not to give the audience encouragement when he has a chance to recite".

1936 was a year in which politicians and businessmen alike could not please. Unemployed marchers from Jarrow to London were in no mood for amusement and all waved threateningly. Backstage in the spring, Stanley and all the cast discussed the Olympic Games to be held in Berlin. In spite of frequent unsubstantiated rumours about a re-emergent German nation under Adolf Hitler, world news correspondents could enter Berlin freely. As well as reporting how the games were organised they could also comment on signs of the Third Reich developing. There was full employment in Germany. New autobahns were being constructed. Giant silver zeppelins with their red and black swastika emblems, regularly safely flew around the world, were on view to the public. The leaders of Aryan power were pleased with strong athletic examples like Max Schmeling, the heavyweight boxer, for beating Joe Louis, the Brown Bomber from the United States. Hitler would not shake hands with Jesse Owens though the American won four gold medals for sprinting.

In occasional cabaret appearances at the Savoy Hotel, Stanley found out that the doorman

E.L. Martin remembered him from their time serving in the Flanders trenches. Martin was glad Stanley was leading such a full life and had entertained so many people in the last fifteen years.

CHAPTER SEVEN

Trying times.

In 1937, Queenie, Stanley's 45 years old wife, died unfortunately in very distressing circumstances. Stanley said he had enjoyed 24 years of contented married life with a good woman and their four children - Joan, Patricia, John and Mary. At times, life was more difficult because Queenie did not particularly relish the company of show business people. She preferred the outdoor life and horse riding but she placidly accepted the style of her husband's work and it being now considered a worthwhile career.

The trouble had started in 1915, when payments of the £400 to £500 per annum from property rental ceased. Queenie did not write to her husband Lieutenant Holloway in France about this. He had big enough problems of his own fighting in the Front line against the Germans. Queenie unwisely borrowed what she needed from a moneylender and ran deeply into debt over the repayments. She tried to ease her worried thoughts by drinking alcohol. Stanley was shocked to discover the two situations on his return. Though he sorted out their finances, the drinking habit could not be broken. Irreparable harm had been done to Queenie's health.

After the funeral, consoling and making caring arrangements for the children, Stanley immersed himself in his work. He found some moments of light relief with theatrical friends. The role of hearty actor, singer, entertainer, like the show, must go on and grief hidden. Friends were laying small bets on the Derby at Epsom - *Mid Day Sun* seemed a good tip or flutter on the race. The popular amusing song - "Mad dogs and English men go out in the mid day sun", had been written, by the all-round performer, composer, producer and artist Noel Coward, on a trip to the Far East. He joked about how the British reacted to tropical climates. Stanley sang some of Noel's songs.

Laws were introduced at last after the war, prohibiting horse drawn traffic in most of London's West End streets. Stanley watched the football Cup Final at Wembley Stadium. Carter, not a wagon driver, led his out team, in red and white stripes. Presumably his parents named him Horatio after Lord Nelson or the Roman hero who held the bridge. Horatio Carter was a skilful brave genius at football, masterminding a 3-1 victory over 'Proud' Preston North End and is recorded as a hero

King George V had died in 1936. His son Edward, groomed for the throne in difficult times, had visited unemployed coal miners, and met Hitler during the rising power of the Nazi's. The Prince of Wales solemnly announced his abdication because Parliament and Church would not sanction his wedding as monarch to the divorced American woman Mrs Wallace Simpson. Edward slipped quietly away with her into exile. In 1937, the Duke of York was crowned King George VI. His Duchess, Lady Bowes-Lyon, became Queen of England. Their daughter Elizabeth was the heiress to the throne.

Other news Stanley heard on the radio was that new giant Cunard 80,000 ton liner Queen Mary had set out on her transatlantic maiden voyage. Another more startling item was

67

that the German passenger airship Hindenburg had crashed. Airships provided a quicker, quieter travel service to North America though they carried far fewer people than a liner. Newspapers carried horrendous photographs of the blazing inferno at the Lakenhurst mooring mast in New Jersey. The possibility of sabotage was looked into.

Stanley was required to make a film about Sam Small. It was at one of Billy Butlin's new innovative holiday camps. A week's holiday with organised activities was offered for a week's pay. Stanley also made a promotional record "Penny on the Drum" for Butlin's, with Percival Mackey and his band playing.

Stanley had very limited experience of making a silent film, 'The Rotters', in 1921. He didn't particularly see much future in it for him. The advice he received from Gracie Fields in 1934 was about his choice of stage work. Another film - 'D'ye Ken John Peel' in 1935 was a bit more interesting as sound techniques were improving. A film version of the radio show 'In Town Tonight' referred to on page 64, just made for a little variety in his regular work on stage. Stanley and other famous people were seen in ordinary clothes without make-up or costume. This naturalness endeared them more to the public and Stanley only realised in retrospect, how much perhaps this and the other small parts in films, helped him during these difficult years of bereavement. They had given him some experience for what was to follow and kept his name before the public.

In 1938, Stanley made the acquaintance at Twickenham Film Studios of Violet Marion Lane. She was a twenty year old young actress, film extra, chorus artist from Leeds and daughter of a civil engineer. Good company, it was easy her having a true Yorkshire dialect, to skilfully imitate his north country voice for their amusement.

Larry Adler met Stanley at a recording studio and congratulated him for making 12

68

records. These sold for 6/- (30p), providing a useful royalty. Adler was so talented an harmonica player that Vaughan Williams and other composers wrote serious pieces for mouth organ. Record sales of Stanley singing popular songs and reciting monologues were good. However Stanley had a different repertoire from the Australian Peter Dawson. After making his debut with Henry Wood at the Promenade Concerts at Queens Hall, Dawson went on to sing at Covent Garden opera house and recorded 3,000 songs.

A year later, when making a film at Ealing Studios Stanley again met Laney, as Violet Lane was known. She supported him by travelling up to Birmingham to see him playing Abanazar in the pantomime *Aladdin*. Laney and Stanley were very good company for each other. He was however 48 and a little concerned about the difference in their ages.

The 2nd January 1939 was a happy New Year. Stanley married Violet Marion Lane in Manchester. As Clacton had been the venue for his first wedding, Stanley said he didn't go in for glamorous places! The second wedding was a quiet ecumenical ceremony at the Registry Office. A Jewish stage manager and chauffeur witnessed the legal contract of a protestant and non practising catholic!. The couple went round to the Midland Hotel for a reception. The only guests were Emile Littler the impresario and his pantomime (principal boy) wife Cora Coffin. There was no publicity or cameraman although people at the theatre knew of the wedding. Three weeks later a reporter from the Evening Standard asked Stanley to confirm or deny the rumour he was remarried. Stanley wasn't on the best of terms with the Press at that time, over a review they had printed about the show. He did however supply them with the the details of his wedding and his dear wife. Stanley said Laney was a wonderful stepmother for his teenage children.

Stanley enthusiastically resumed his career. In a variety show at the Holborn Empire in

69

February, twice nightly, Stanley Holloway, star of stage, screen and radio, amused London audiences. Tom Mix, (a famous cowboy of films), Teddy Brown, xylophonist - (the massive man with the light touch) and pianist Norman Long (with a smile and a song), made up a good programme.

'Co-Operette' was a film Stanley helped make. Nobody could have really anticipated the lack of political co-operation and the momentous turn of events later in the year. The visit to Hitler in Munich the previous year, by Neville Chamberlain, the Prime Minister and former Lord Mayor of Birmingham, had apparently achieved some agreement. The German invasion of Czechoslovakia, after annexing Sudetenland and voraciously extending their boundaries, made it clear Chamberlain's Munich agreement was not worth the paper it was written on. Britain declared war again against Germany on 3rd September.

Stanley, Laney and the stepchildren took air raid precautions, blacked out windows and sheltered in the Anderson, listening to news bulletins and for the wail of sirens.

CHAPTER EIGHT

Life on the silver screen.

Looking back over the pattern of time, places and parts Stanley had in films, his career began in 1921. He was recalled in 1934 as him name was becoming more widely known through theatre and radio appearances. He made four significant films each in the years 1934, 1935 and 1937. He like the British film industry did not expand until 1944 when some floodgates other than the Mohne dam ones, opened and he was kept very busy for 10 years in good supporting roles, occasionally co-starring. For a further ten years he averaged a film annually until the amazing hit when he was 74.

Fox Talbot's work in Britain was continuing in parallel by R.W. Paul Auguste Lumiere in France, with his cinematographe and by Latham in the U.S.A. Films at first were only of a few minutes duration. As skills were discovered, *The Birth of a Nation'* was made in America. Directed by D.W. Griffith this silent film is recognised as a classic production. His Biograph drew together in 1919 Charlie Chaplin, Mary Pickford and Douglas Fairbanks to found United Artists and focus the industry in Hollywood.

The early postwar silent films were an amazing experience for the audience. The novelty of moving pictures was included in some part of music hall shows and Stanley saw and wondered at the flickering views on the screen. Cinemas were soon springing up everywhere to surpass and oust the attraction of live performances even by celebrities. A pianist at first and later an organist, played appropriate mood music to try to fit the activity on the screen.

In 1921, although aged 31, Stanley played his first part in a film. *'The Rotters'* PLOT: it was a comedy silent film set in a school. The headmistress recognises the Justice of the Peace as her ex lover. She persuades him not to pass sentence on the mayor's son. CAST: Arthur Wait - Stanley, John Clugson, M.P. - Sydney Paxton, Estelle Clugson - Margery Meadows, John Wait - Ernest English and Jemima Nivet - Sydney Fairbrother. For this juvenile part, Stanley was paid £5 a day for the two weeks it took to make. Apparently Stanley hadn't then the potential of a Rudolph Valentino or Fairbanks.

Demands for shows by *The Co-Optimists* and others waned in popularity as the novelty visual antics thrived. In 1927 too, Al Jolson arrived with talking pictures in *'The Jazz Singer'*. As cinemas and facilities for soundtracks increased, so the unemployment

71

of many pianists grew, who had accompanied silent movies. There are some film archive examples of Stanley Holloway with the *Co-Optimists* in 1930, helping with trial experiments to perfect a sound track for Visatone. Critics thought the script directed by Edwin Greenwood for   New Era Company was poor, missing the opportunity of showing the story from foundation of idea to the first night of the troupe at the Royalty theatre.

Stanley felt he was a late starter at being cast in films but now at last he was noticed and began to get small character parts. He appeared in *'Sleeping Car' in 1932* starring Ivor Novello and Madeline Carrol. PLOT: Set in France, a woman on the run marries a sleeping car attendant to avoid the police. It was directed by Litvak for Gaumont British. CAST: Stanley - Francois, Kay Hammond- Simone and Laddie Cliff - Pierre.

'The Girl from Maxim's' was a play by Georges Feydeau. PLOT: a doctor passes a singer off as his wife. Made by United Artists the CAST: included Stanley as Mongincourt, la Morne, a Night Club singer - Frances Day and Dr. Petypon - Leslie Henson A talented young film producer/director named Alexander Korda directed this farce. Some of the film was shot on location in Paris at the Pathe Nathan studios.

Stanley's next work under the lights and cameras was in 1934. It was a pleasant change for Stanley to be in a film again. Maurice Elvey, the producer of Warner Brothers studio at Burbank, came to Twickenham studios to make - *'The Lily of Killarney* or as issued in the U.S.A. - *' Bride of the Lake'* from play The Colleen Bawn. PLOT: A peasant is kidnapped by a smuggler. A knight is implicated. CAST: Father O'Flynn - Stanley Holloway, Sir James Corrigan - Leslie Perrins,

Sir Patrick Cregeen - John Garrick, Gina Malo - Eileen O'Connor,

Miles-na-Coppaleen -Dennis Hoey and Pamela May - Ann Chute

A comedy film directed by Paul Merzbach followed - *'Love at Second Sight'*
or The Girl Thief'.

PLOT: A match king's daughter pretends to love the inventor of an everlasting match.

CAST: Marian Marsh - Juliet, Anthony Bushell - Bill, Supporting were Neil Kenyon,

Claude Hulbert - Alan Parsley, , Ralph Ince - McIntosh, Joan Gardiner - Evelyn,

Stanley - Policeman again!.

In the evolving cinema industry, the danger of type casting someone was not initially seen
as a potential problem. Stanley had travelled for filming at Blackpool on weekends in 1934
during the stage show *Three Sisters*. As he was Police Constable Eustace Titherley in the
show, naturally Basil Dean wanted Stanley for a bobby in the 1934 film *'Sing as We Go'*.

PLOT: A mill girl tries various jobs
at Blackpool.
CAST: Gracie Fields - Gracie Platt,
Dorothy Hyson   - Phyllis Logan,
John Loder -   Hugh Philips,
Frank Pettingell - Murgatroyd Platt,
Policeman   - Stanley Holloway.
Gracie Fields was becoming a legend
Her Lancashire national anthem
was - "Sally, pride of our alley".

Later, broadcaster Alistair Cooke in his 'Letter from America' said "If you ask anyone to sum up Lancashire in two words, it was a girl from a Rochdale mill town with no claim to vocal purity or power, only a brassy beguiling honesty - Gracie Fields".

Stanley was off duty from filming on location where, as a policeman he had controlled traffic on the Preston Rd. Bystanders saw him, still in police uniform and mistaking him for a real official, asked for directions to the nearest public convenience! He was obviously as convincing as the model inside Madame Tussaud's Waxworks exhibition in Marylebone Road. As a boy I and many others have unknowingly asked that policeman a question!

The next musical film setting for Stanley was, at the end of 1934, in '*Road House*' directed again by Maurice Elvey for Gaumont.

In the PLOT: A murderer is tracked down by Donovan and a barmaid.

CAST: Donovan - Stanley Holloway, Chester - Emlyn Williams, Sam Pritchard - Gordon Harker, Belle Tout - Violet Loraine, Lady Hamble - Marie Lohr.

Stanley, with five, more significant films behind him, was invited in 1935, to appear in '*D'ye Ken John Peel*' another musical. Directed by Julius Hagen it would be known in the U.S.A. as '*Captain Moonlight*'. A nucleus of cast kept reappearing in different parts.

PLOT: Army major falls in love with a married woman. He exposes her husband as a bigamous gambler. CAST: several of whom Stanley had worked with before Maj. John Peel, John Garrick, Lucy Merrall (not Meryll from G. & S. '*Yeomen of guard!*') - Winifred Shotter, Captain Moonlight - John Stuart and Toinette - Mary Lawson.

(It would have been better made in colour so that the pink coats could be seen).

The huntsman's song suited Stanley - "*Peel's view hello to awaken the dead and the fox from his lair in the morning!*".

74

Stanley was able to be himself when a film was made of the radio programme -
'In Town Tonight'. PLOT: In this revue, and agent tries to find stars to make records.
CAST: Manager - Finlay Currie, Agent - Jack Barty. Various stars are interviewed -
Wilson, Betty and Keppel, the unusual music hall dancers, Stanley Holloway, Olive Groves,
the Tiller Girls, Beryl Orde, Bob Lively and Kneller Hall military band add music.
The the traffic is stopped by a policeman and Stanley had an interesting interview.
The part of a policeman has been played by plenty of other actors e.g. Jack Buchanan,
Laurence Olivier, Will Hay, Rob Wilton etc. They have donned the distinctive blue serge
uniform of Law and Order at sometime in their career, to convey the impression of authority.

It was fourth time lucky perhaps for Stanley as a policeman in the film *Squibs* in 1934.
PLOT:- A gambler's flower seller daughter wins a sweepstake and marries a policemen.
CAST: Sam Hopkins - Gordon Harker, Squibs Hopkins - Betty Balfour, Inspector Lee -
Morris Harvey, P.C. Charley Lee - Stanley, Bill - Ronald Shiner.
In the film, Stanley married a cockney girl selling flowers in Covent Garden.(Did this
unknowingly predict like - 'The Shape of Things to Come', music Arthur Bliss had just
written for the soundtrack of a film with that title!) that twenty years hence another even
more important cockney flower girl would enter Stanley's life?

Other films at that time in which Stanley had parts were:- *Play up the band*.
PLOT: A euphonium player visits the Crystal Palace and becomes tangled up in a theft.
CAST: Sam Small - Stanley Holloway, Betty Small - Betty Ann Davies, Lord Heckdyke -
Charles Sewell, Lady Heckdyke - Amy Veness, and Alf Ramsbottom - Frank Atkinson
With Ramsbottoms and Smalls, Stanley's characters were given a different treatment.

'Song of the forge' and 'The Village Blacksmith' is a musical directed by Henry Edwards.

PLOT: A son doesn't *follow in father's footsteps* but goes into the car business.

CAST: Davy Burnaby - Auctioneer (nice to meet up with an old Co-Ops pal six years later)

C. Denier Warren - Farmer George, (a popular radio broadcaster), Clerk - Mervyn Johns,

Eleanor Faye, and, heading the cast - Joe/Sir William Barrett - Stanley Holloway.

His build and hearty voice obviously fitted the role of wielding a hammer shoeing horses.

Stanley's current experience on film sets was now enough for producer Julius Hagen and

director Henry Edwards to cast him for the most important part he had been asked to play so

far, the title role of an Irish priest in *'The Vicar of Bray'*. It was filmed at Twickenham

Riverside Studios, Hammersmith in west London, and directed by Henry Edwards.

PLOT: A priest goes to London as tutor to Prince Charles. When Charles regains the throne

he keeps a promise to the priest and frees a man condemned to death.

CAST: The Vicar of Bray - Stanley Holloway, Earl of Brendon -Felix Aylmer,

Dennis Melross - Esmond Knight Lady Brendon - Margaret Vines, Sir Richard Melross -

Garry Marsh, King Charles - Hugh Miller and Prince Charles Stuart - Hamilton Price,

An unsympathetically severe critic of a 1990's re-run on television, said

disparagingly of this dip into archives, - 'The Vicar of Bray' - "Mercifully the kind of film

they don't make any more. It is not without moments of interest as an historical artefact but

the songs are ghastly, the period trappings cheap and inaccurate. Felix Aylmer is

satisfactory." Even with of a fraction of the enormous budgets spent today in filming, neither

the cast nor the cameras could have possibly done much better in 1937. The film was very

good for its time and stage of development of techniques. The film industry could hardly run before it walked. Some expensive modern films can leave viewers with worse feelings.

Unlike a part on the stage or in a concert hall, in making films or gramophone records there is no audience to react to. In films the complete story is divided up into scenes. These are then shot in any convenient order to make the most economical use of location, light, make-up costume and artist. It harder for the cast to keep in character and mood.

The Visatone soundtrack system was one of the most advanced of its kind. Sound crews were learning to work unobtrusively with early microphones. Known tunes added to emotive background for stories, just as the piano tried to in the days of silent films. In the *Vicar of Bray*, melodies - 'The Lark in the Clear Air' by S. Ferguson and 'The last Rose of Summer' by Thomas Moore fitted the story quite well. Stanley's three solos, were sung in a street scene or at the inn. With only some film extras pretending to be listening on the artificial set, it is harder to give a convincing performance than in a theatre or concert hall with a live audience. Seeing it now shows too that with having to maintain an Irish brogue, some voice quality may be lost. However, "Dear auld Ireland in the Mornin",

"Down Among the Dead Men" and the title song are fine -
"In good King Charles's golden days when loyalty no harm meant,
a zealous high church man was I and learned to get preferment
but this is law and I'll maintain until my dying day sir
yet whatsoe're a king may reign still I'll be the Vicar of Bray."

In these films Stanley had renewed acquaintance with Davy Burnaby, Laddie Cliff and Violet Loraine recalling happy times with the *Co-Ops*. Leslie Henson, George Grossmith and Esmond Knight, Stanley had also appeared with before in the theatre. Austin Melford, another of Stanley's friends in the *Co-optimists*, had also moved on from

77

that apprenticeship and become a successful filmscript writer.

In 1937, before a lull in his being screened, Stanley was given a part in a Gaumont British/Independent film directed by Bernard Vorhaus. *'Cotton Queen or Crying out loud'*.
PLOT: - Two strongly competing millowners overcome their disagreements to co-operate after novelist daughter poses as worker in rival's mill.
CAST: - Bob Todcastle - Will Fyffe, Sam Owen - Stanley Holloway, Joan - Mary Lawson, Helen Haye - Margaret Owen and Johnny Owen - Jimmy Hanley.
In the course of the film Stanley has to appear to be drunk and stagger around. Co -star Will Fyffe was more used to such roles with his signature tune on the Music Halls - 'I belong to Glasgow'. He will always be remembered by Scots and others for singing - "When I get a couple of drinks on a Saturday Glasgow belongs to me!"

'Sam Small leaves town', was a film in black and white, produced by M.F. Wilson. at the end of, 1937, took Stanley briefly out of his problems at home.
PLOT: A famous actor is bet by a publisher he cannot disappear for a week. Manning swaps with Sam Small, a jack of all trades at an holiday camp. In the end he allows himself to be discovered by a young reporter, and wins a reward and can afford to marry his girlfriend.
CAST: Manning - Stanley Holloway.
Critics thought the running time of eighty minutes for the film was too long.

Cartoon films were made with Stanley's dialogue. *'Threehapence* a foot', 'Sam's Medals' 'Alt who goes there', 'Beat the retreat', and 'Sam on sentry duty at Buckingham Palace'
These were useful as shorts before advertisements and interval after which the main feature was shown. Stanley was in 'Our Island Nation' a publicity/propaganda film.

After the year in which his wife Queenie died, Stanley spent some time away from cameras. He was recalled for 'Co-Operette', a film with better screenplay showing the rise and success of the Co-Optimists. Then came his remarriage to Laney just before the war

In May, back on stage, he shared top of the bill at the Empire Theatre, Nottingham, with Nellie Wallace the 'Queen of Low comedy or Essence of Eccentricity' as she was variably called. When reminiscing Stanley commented her exaggerated style of performance was styled grotesque, not like his South American troupe. Though not a completely unattractive woman offstage, Nellie dressed and behaved awkwardly in her act.

Nellie Wallace's deliberately crude style music hall turn was remembered by Richard Baker, the B.B.C. announcer and music enthusiast. As a boy he saw her at the Metropolitan in the Edgware Road. She sang such songs as "My mother said always look under the bed, before you blow the candle out to see if there's a man about" and "He's gone afar to Afrikee much farther than he went with me!".

At Nottingham, Stanley remembered her being fastidious over cleanliness. Nellie sprayed the dressing room and toilet with fly killer and lavender water, saying in a high pitched querulous voice "Oh dear the filthy beasts!". She was the opitomy of an eccentric music hall artist. This strange incongruous character, often appeared in high

Nellie Wallace

buttoned black boots. She wore a battered trilby hat and a moth eaten, mangy bit of fur, her 'bit of vermin'. At other times Nellie, dressed as a washerwoman, would coyly make frivolous comments about frilly underwear. A young boy in a Coliseum audience was impressed by her. He remembered her green dress. In a nurse's uniform standing behind a screen, her silhouette appeared to be assisting an operating surgeon. A hot water bottle, flat iron and chicken were surprisingly removed from the stomach of the patient! The boy did not really understand why the rest of the audience were convulsed with laughter at her words and humorous actions. Instead of buying an ice cream at the interval he handed a few yellow roses and a thank you note in at the stage door, to be taken to Nellie Wallace's dressing room. A few weeks later when the young boy was ill in bed with a high temperature, a bouquet of yellow roses arrived with a note from Nellie 'for the little boy who sent the roses. 'Get well soon'. That little boy was Alec Guinness! It showed him how surprisingly kind, caring and human   in fact Nellie Wallace was. She managed something else different too. The dame at the pantomime tradition is usually played by a man and the principal boy by a woman. Nellie was the witch in *Sleeping Beauty* and was surprisingly asked to replace George Robey as Dame Trot in *Jack and the Beanstalk!*

Just as Ian Wallace later recalled clearly seeing Stanley Holloway perform at Golders Green Hippodrome, Stanley remembered seeing earlier, Marie Lloyd and George Lashwood at music halls. These further admitted memories by younger Richard Baker and Sir Alec Guinness, about Nellie Wallace, seem to say something of the effect live performers can have. Could she have been an influence on others in their choice of a career?

CHAPTER NINE

Royal approval.

Royal patronage acknowledging theatre artists is welcomed by the profession. While there have been entertainers at court throughout history, perhaps Queen Victoria set standards for the attitudes of 20th century monarchs towards popular entertainment. It was she who asked Sir Arthur Sullivan to provide some musical relaxation for the royal household at Windsor on 6th March 1891. He expected her serene, reputedly dour, Majesty (still mourning the loss of her beloved consort Prince Albert), to have him conduct excerpts from his serious works - 'The Tempest', 'The Prodigal Son', 'The Golden legend' or 'Ivanhoe'. However, she surprised him by asking for the GONDOLIERS! This pleased W.S. Gilbert who hadn't been knighted and felt his words were not given the recognition they deserved. Her Majesty had heard and was obviously amused at the idea of a monarch "Rising early in the morning and proceed to light the fire! - before polishing off some political despatches and running little errands for ministers of state!". The public had been shown in fun, and now perhaps realised, that being royal could have some disadvantages.

After Queen Victoria died, King George V in 1912 continued to enlighten royalty by agreeing to have and attend the first Royal Command Performance. George Robey 'The Prime Minister of Mirth' was invited but not the much loved 'Queen of the Halls', Marie Lloyd, It was thought, said Stanley, that she might refer, as she often did, to something crude like powdering a baby's bottom. Anything so shocking or risque could offend the royal party. Marie's pride suffered a bit but she packed the nearby London Pavilion theatre with the notice -*"Marie Lloyd gives a command performance every night!"*.

Informal visits to the theatre by royalty raised the morale of the cast and company.

81

Stanley saw Lady Elizabeth Bowes-Lyon attending   the Prince of Wales Theatre in 1922. It was apparently a birthday treat for the young Duke of Kent. During the *Co-Optimists'* show, he left his seat in the Royal Box. Somehow he had heard that Davy Burnaby would go on stage dressed as Britannia, playing a trumpet! Stagehands pelted Davy with harmless imitation bricks. His Royal Highness was seen in the wings enthusiastically helping them! Stanley sang "Rule Britannia" but with a variation of the chorus "Britons never never never shall be *mar-ri-ed to a mer-mi-aid* at the bottom of the deep blue sea!".

When Lady Bowes-Lyon became engaged and then Duchess of York in 1923, she attended a cabaret at the Dorchester Hotel organised by Gerald du Maurier. The Royal party were sitting quite close to where Stanley performed. He noticed that during his recitation of the Lion and Albert monologue, when he first mentioned Albert, the Duchess appeared to give the Duke a nudge. He thought it was because His Royal Highness Prince George's second name was Albert.

In 1925, at a colourful gala royal show Stanley sang/spoke a Greatrix Newman monologue - "The king who wanted jam for tea". It again suggested omnipotence could have some problems. The idea may have come from the writer A.A. Milne who published a poem about Christopher Robin and Alice, watching the changing of the guard at Buckingham Palace. The trend, of occasionally mentioning royalty in amusing circumstances, continued and the Duke and Duchess of York again enjoyed the show.

Stanley always treasured the memory of a small tea party given by Queen Mary at Buckingham Palace. He had recited the monologue "Alt ! who goes there!" in which Sam has tea with the queen who asks him how many lumps of sugar he would like. Afterwards Queen Mary congratulated Stanley adding with a smile" But I'm afraid I don't pour the tea myself here". He recounted this occasion later on the radio show 'Holloway for

Laughter'. On another occasion at Her Majesty's Theatre he thought Queen Mary leaned to

one side of the Royal Box to hide some of her laughter. It might still be considered unseemly

by some, for her to appear to be too affected by the humour, in front of the public.

In 1933, Mabel Constanduros, who had appeared with Stanley in a film, wrote

"Old Sam's Party" for him. In the recitation, Sam Small, nearly eighty, has a Christmas

party. Well known characters from musket days are invited. King George the Fourth and the

Queen drop in for a cup of tea. "They hung up their crowns on the stand in the hall, Sam paid

off their cab eighteen pence. The Queen parked her mace in Sam's umbrella stand, 'now' she

said 'let party commence!' ".

It was in April 1935 that Stanley had learned to recite with Godfrey Tearle's help -

"This royal throne of king this sceptered isle, this earth this majesty this seat of Mars

This other Eden, demi paradise, this fortress built by nature for herself against infection

and the hand of war. This happy breed of men, this little world, this precious stone

set in a silver sea which serves it the office of a wall or as a moat defensive to a house,

against the envy of less happier lands; This blessed plot, this earth, this realm, this England".

The 'good luck' wish over the phone from Godfrey, for Stanley's first Shakespeare piece in

'Life begins at Oxford Circus' at the Palladium in the Spring of 1935, soon came true.

From 6th October 1935, Stanley was at the Empire theatre, Edinburgh. A reporter said

"Crowded houses greeted Stanley Holloway. It was with reluctance he was allowed to

make a final bow after an act which included many of his famous characters. Mr. Holloway's

reception was of unusual warmth". The show was directed by George Black. He was also

given an even bigger responsibility with the royal show at the end of the month.

83

On 29th October 1935, at the Palladium, over £5,000 was raised for the Variety Artists Benevolent Fund at the Royal Performance arranged by George Black and Harry Marlow. King George V and Queen Mary attended the commemoration of the silver jubilee of the opening of the music hall theatre in 1910. The Stage reporter wrote: " Stanley Holloway took to the Palladium stage, with Wolseley Charles at the piano. From his gallery of Albert studies he chose that one from Marriott Edgar's pen which told of the young Lancastrian's adventures with a Jubilee Sovereign. This a gem of a number showed Mr. Holloway in his best form. A Chevalier impersonation followed and then 'Brown Boots', a sketch concerning the worthy wearer of unworthy 'brahn' boots at a funeral, with just a touch of sentiment and an opportunity for Mr. Holloway to display that fine baritone voice of which one would willingly have heard more." The Daily Mail review the next day said - "Mr. Stanley Holloway, in his best north country accent, contributed another escapade of young Albert Ramsbottom who this time swallows a Jubilee Sovereign."

Later in the programme the reporter for The Stage noted "Will Mahoney 'stopped the programme', that is to say applause for him continued after Stanley Holloway had appeared to announce the next turn. Mr Holloway eventually secured possession of the stage to introduce a group of performers of fifty years ago."

The curtains were drawn and there on the Palladium stage sat the residents of Brinsworth Home for Aged Artists. What a cheer they received from the surprised audience. Stanley introduced Frank Bertram, aged 94, who had rung his handbells for Queen Victoria at Osborne House. This 'Cavalcade of Variety' by the O.A.P's was a very day out for them. Travelling at 9a.m. from Twickenham, many wore carefully preserved costumes. Their combined ages totalled 2,304 years but they certainly weren't *Old Contemptibles.*

Unlike Chelsea pensioners on parade they were grouped on stage with some stars of a later school like Nervo and Knox, Naughton and Gold and Flanagan and Allen. Stanley announced the veteran entertainers as - "Stars of 25 years ago and still star performers today, taking it in turns to introduce numbers which have long been associated with their names". Miss Kate Carney dressed in her Pearly Queen costume sang "Are we to part like this" and "Three pots a shilling". Next Mr. Gus Elen sang "Down the road away went Polly" and he was followed by Miss Florrie Forde whose ageing voice still thundered out bravely "Down at the old Bull and Bush" and "Pack up your troubles". Lastly as grand as ever" Stanley introduced - Mr. Harry Champion who sang in his inimitable raucous cockney way - "Boiled Beef and carrots" and "Any old iron".

Florrie Forde surprised Stanley after this memorable royal show by asking him if he liked crabs?! When he said yes she invited him to her dressing room where she had a quantity of them. They sat reminiscing together literally *breaking a leg,* happily munching. They wondered why Eugene Stratton had not been invited. His famous soft shoe dance routine, he did so well whilst singing "She's my lady love, she is my Lily of Laguna, she is my lily and my rose", was conspicuously absent. The public were told that he was unfortunately too ill to attend. About censorship some people thought that the Lord Chamberlain's representatives seemed surprisingly more strict in the east than in the west End of London.

After the abdication of King Edward the VII and coronation of King George VI in 1936, the new King and Queen attended a show where Stanley was performing and requested 'Sam and his musket' be recited. At the backstage presentation, the Queen Mother wished Stanley good luck in pantomime. He thought it was typically caring and courteous of her.

She had apparently taken the trouble to find out he was appearing as Abanazar again in *Aladdin* at Golders Green two months later.

In 1937, Bush radio used 'The king with the terrible temper' monologue for publicity. In 1938 Hanson's coffee essence had Sam in patriotic Red, white and blue sales promotion. The British cartoons with famous Sam and Albert characters appeared on pottery as well as in print. Another treasured royal memory for Stanley was when he first appeared before the daughters of the Queen. The young Princesses Elizabeth and Margaret listened to his 'Signalman Sam'. Whenever he did this monologue he invited the audience to join in the chorus saying in the rhythm of a train "Fish and chips, fish and chips". The Royal family at Windsor joined in.

The greatest moment in any artist's life is to attend Buckingham Palace, to receive an award in recognition of their professional contribution to entertainment in the United Kingdom. Stanley Holloway was so honoured on the 24th February, 1960.

When Her Majesty Queen Elizabeth was respectfully reminded by me in her seventieth year of former meetings with the fine character, the late Stanley Holloway, O.B.E., she kindly graciously instructed the following reply be sent:-

BUCKINGHAM PALACE

9th April, 1996.

Dear Mr Walding.

I am commanded by The Queen to write and thank you for your letter with its entertaining anecdotes of the late Stanley Holloway, O.B.E. Her Majesty was most interested to read of your researches into Theatrical Heritage and she wishes you well in this project.

I am to thank you again for writing and for telling The Queen the amusing stories about Stanley Holloway of whom she has very happy memories.

Yours sincerely

Henrietta Abel Smith

Lady-in-Waiting

R. Walding, Esq.

CHAPTER TEN

The second front.

Stanley made many radio broadcasts for the B.B.C. in the late 1930's, after the death of his wife Queenie and before his remarriage to Laney. Harry S. Pepper, Stanley's former colleague in the Co-Optimists who had transferred to B.B.C. productions, organised a White Coon Show and asked Stanley to appear. At rehearsal Stanley sang "With her head tucked underneath her arm", a popular monologue written by Weston and Lee. When Stanley used the words " Bloody Tower" it was thought the watchdog censor would not allow these to be broadcast. Roy Eckersley, who had risen from disc jockey to director, recently replaced by Doris Arnold with 'These you have loved', was called upon to decide. Stanley convinced Roy the words were used as a noun and part of a well known name as the history of the Tower of London. It was allowed to be heard. Under B.B.C non commercial policies, could he be allowed to say - "With a stick with an 'orse's 'ead 'andle, the finest *Woolworth's* could sell"?

At the London Palladium early in 1938 the show *London Rhapsody* was reported in the News of the World on 6th February " to be without question, George Black's greatest achievement." CAST: Flanagan and Allen had another hit song "Run rabbit run". Supported by - Naughton and Gold, Raymond Newell and the Budapest Gypsy Boys. Stanley was invited to join in on the 4th April. He remembered the jokes they played on each other. Even comedy routines become a bit monotonous after many weeks. On one occasion he had to come offstage to change quickly for the next sketch. The set for this was Piccadilly where Stanley was acting as a woman flower seller. Suitably attired, Stanley hurriedly grabbed his basket of flowers. He couldn't pick it up! It weighed a ton! He did eventually struggle on it and learned later that Jimmy Nervo had filled it with weights.

Artists occasionally resorted to such pranks and tested each others reactions to not having ideal conditions, as they performed in front of an audience. No minor problem should throw a professional. After two months larking about with these fine entertainers Stanley went on tour in another revue *All the Best*.

In 1939, at the Holborn Empire, Stanley did his turn singing and reciting monologues. Cowboy, Tom Mix and sparkling xylophonist, Teddy Brown, were again in the cast.

In September 1939, Prime Minister Nevil Chamberlain's non aggression pact failed. Hitler's Nazi Germany invaded Poland and war was declared. On the radio it was announced that all theatres and public meeting places were closed for the duration in the interests of public safety. When the expected air raids did not start, Londoners were , lulled temporarily into a false sense of security. Some theatres, cinemas and halls were allowed to reopen for matinee performances. Stanley said this chance helped reconcile the need for the public to relax from being constantly vigilant at night (in case of enemy attacks).

Myra Hess gave lunch hour concerts at the National Gallery in Trafalgar Square as another way of keeping up morale. A young Joyce Grenfell helped make   sandwich refreshments. Once an unexploded bomb, which had fallen in the night in another part of the building, went off during the recital. Myra Hess played on as though nothing had happened.

There were many such stories of bravery. Noel Coward coming out of an Air Raid shelter one morning, noticed a common little flower and wrote the song "London Pride". During the *phoney wartime* as it was called, Stanley made many more recordings of monologues and songs which were played at the speed of 78 revolutions per minute.

At home at Luton, Beds, aged eight, living a quarter of a mile away from the Vauxhall

Motors factory, I spent many nights in the Anderson Shelter. My two brothers and three sisters had all helped dig the hole at the end of the garden and cover over the corrugated metal. There was some bombing by aircraft that had strayed 30 miles north of London and other raids in daylight, trying to stop the manufacture of Bedford lorries and Churchill tanks.

To further boost public morale for the increasingly harassed Londoners, a show was arranged at the Saville Theatre in April, 1940. It was called *Up and Doing*. Leslie Henson was co-producer and appeared with Stanley in a very funny sketch in the second half. This a parody, by Reginald Purdell, of a dramatic monologue written by Milton Hayes - 'The Green Eye of the Little Yellow God'   was renamed - 'Pukka Sahib - the elocutionist'.

Leslie Henson appeared as a colonel and Cyril Richard, as a major. They sat in uniform in a box seats as part of the audience.
Stanley came on and began to recite in serious tone -
There's a green eyed yellow idol to the north of Khatmandu There's a little marble cross below the town, There's a..."

(Here the Colonel loudly interrupted by asking his colleague "Have you been there lately?" Their discussion explains the town is much changed since the description was written.)
Stanley starts again amending "A little marble cross *above* the town."
Numerous other interruptions occur and Stanley restarts several times until, in the end, he

rushed madly off the stage! This 'Pukka Sahibs' sketch was considered to be a comedy classic. As with the flower basket trick, Henson and Richard, sometimes during the show changed questions to catch Stanley out. He was equally adept at modifying his answers.

As his own contribution to the war effort Stanley wrote and used a topical monologue:- 'Albert Evacuated'. It was about Mr.Ramsbottom instructing girls in First Aid.
Marriott Edgar was rather unhappy at not being consulted over this one. Stanley also wrote with Graham John one called 'Careless Talk' and performed it with Leslie Henson. For the National Savings Committee at Merton Park. He appeared briefly on the 441 feet of 35 mm film called 'Albert's Savings'. Stanley wrote and recited a monologue about wartime thrift:-
Little Albert Ramsbottom, to see how much money he'd got,

put a knife in his money box slot hole and fiddled and pulled out the lot.

It amounted to fifteen and fourpence which by a few simple sums was

ninety five tuppeny ices and twice that in penn'orths of gums.

The sound of the counting of money brought father's head round the door

Tha's not going to to spend all that money on toffee and things

just buy a savings certificate and help us to make more guns!

Up and Doing, produced with the limitations of economy was still styled 'A Glamorous Revue'. Carol Gibbons the talented pianist starred in it. As there seemed no likelihood of any shows coming over from America in wartime, George Gershwin, Cole Porter and others kindly allowed some of their songs to be used in British shows. Rogers and Hart had written *The Boys from Syracuse* based on Shakespeare's 'A Comedy of Errors'. A very popular number was borrowed for the revue in London "This can't be love because I feel so well".

A tour of *Up and Doing* was arranged to cheer provincial towns who were suffering from bombing and rationing of food, clothing and petrol. It was much appreciated at the Glasgow

91

Empire as ships on the river Clyde were prime targets for bombing by the Luftwaffe. Stanley in the part of Old Magee, on stage sits at a table in a poor Irish cottage. With a patch over one eye, and playing his fiddle he plaintively sings "A Kerry Courting". Graham Payn and Pat Barber cling to each other in the background.

E.N.S.A. the Entertainments National Service Association had been formed to boost the morale of the soldiers, sailors and airmen. Basil Dean, a film producer, organised E.N.S.A. from an office in Drury Lane, ('Every Night Something Awful', a nickname it lived down). Numerous concerts were arranged at military bases up and down the country. The stages were often very makeshift. At one show for the naval Home Fleet in the Solent, a gentleman was seen, at an entertainment almost rolling in the aisle with laughter at the 'Pukka Sahib' sketch. The headline above a photograph in the Sunday Dispatch the next day read:-
'WHAT MADE THE KING LAUGH AT A NAVY CONCERT?
When His Majesty King George VI as admiral visited his fleet, he found Stanley Holloway, Leslie Henson and Cyril Richard providing hilarious entertainment'.

Entertaining in Manchester in 1940 for Tom Arnold at the Palace Theatre, The Midland Hotel,(where Stanley and Laney had had their small wedding reception in 1939), was still standing after the blitz. Elsie and Doris Waters, Anne Zeigler and Webster Booth, Tommy Trinder, Billy Bennett and Malcolm Sargent were staying there.
Stanley went with the others for safety to the air raid shelters. He recalled sharing the sad emotion with orchestral conductor, Malcolm Sargent, when emerging on the all clear signal, they saw flames pouring from the famous Free Trade Concert Hall. Loudspeakers warned "All water must be boiled". The show must go on if at all possible and did, with morning and afternoon performances, before everyone took to the shelters again for more night raids.

In 1940, the Holloway home was at High Wycombe in Buckinghamshire. There were lovely views over the chalk hills and beech woods from Bledlow Ridge. Stanley sometimes stayed in a flat in New Cavendish Street when working late in London.

The B.B.C. planned a further series of six broadcasts of Stanley's well known voice reciting monologues. It was for the 'Starlight Show' and, transmitted on the Overseas service, could be picked up by troops in North Africa. The show was compered by Freddy Grisewood a well known newscaster whose voice and that of Alvar Liddel were trusted. Listeners to B.B.C. announcements had to be wary of false propaganda information put on the air by Lord Haw Haw. After the war William Joyce, the American/Irish fascist was executed for treason for his misleading information.

Many cinemas were open in day time to give brief respite to the worried overworked people from all walks of life. Somehow, films continued to be made and Stanley Holloway was involved in several of them. At studios special air raid precautions were necessary when locations were floodlit for filming at night. The many screens and voracious cinema audiences played a major part in entertainment. They needed to be busily fed with new stories from the studios. The Odeon, Ritz, Royalty, Gaumont, Rex, Savoy, Palace, Union, Plaza and others had two different shows each week. The programme for relaxation consisted of a short often amusing film followed by 'Pathe' or 'Movietone News' and then the main feature -'Gone with the Wind' with Clark Gable as Rhett Butler and Vivien Leigh as Scarlett O'hara. The monologue 'Brahn Boots' was written by Weston and Lee in 1940. It was accepted in Stanley's repertoire because the British sometimes need to laugh at themselves. The thoughtful way Stanley recited the idea of going to a funeral for Aunt Hannah may have helped some people come to terms with the frequent news of a relation or

93

someone they knew having been killed by bombs or by action in the armed forces. The composer Lionel Bart lived through those times too. Later in *Oliver* there is a song - 'There'll be horses with tall black plumes to escort you to the family tombs".

In his show *Blitz* Bart helps audiences to relive and ease the worst war time experiences.

Producer Gabriel Pascal, at Denham Studios, contacted Stanley in 1941. *Up and Doing* had returned to a Saville Theatre repaired from bomb damage. From April, tired and shocked Londoners, like the show, must go on. A film of Bernard Shaw's *Major Barbara* was made. Stanley was in a minor part as a policeman again. He did have to say a special prologue. The CAST was: Wendy Hiller, in title role, Robert Morley, as an arms tycoon, Sybil Thorndike, Robert Newton and a young Deborah Kerr. Rex Harrison banged loudly on the drum in the Salvation Army band. The film *Major Barbara* reputedly lost £20,000. Stanley however, felt it was this film that put him really in touch with film makers. From enjoying poking fun at the Bernard Shaw story in the 'Co-Optimists' - "The Bandsman's Daughter", Stanley now benefited from a serious approach to the work.

The expenditure of more money and time on films was justified by promoting interest and good feelings for the harassed population. R. Greenwood had written a book - 'Mr. Bunting goes to war'. The film version was - 'Salute John Citizen'.

PLOT: It was a propaganda film showing the world what life was like in wartime. CAST: Stanley played the part of a grumpy Air Raid warden . George Robey appeared in it. He was a good all round actor who undertook any role from Shakespeare to Pantomime. Mabel Constanduros, who had written the 'Old Sam's party' monologue in 1933, for Stanley. bobbed up again as a well known experienced actress. Diana Sheridan, Jimmy Hanley and

94

Peggy Cummings completed the supporting cast.

The B.B.C. asked Stanley at the Maida Vale studios to broadcast a *'Tribute to Tobruk'*. The Eighth army had gallantly held out against Field Marshall Rommel's Africa Corps. Such morale boosting radio programmes were an important part of Stanley's war work. He shared in lunchtime concerts called 'Workers Playtime' at various munition factories.

'Here's Wishing you well' on the radio had a Sam monologue competition. Stanley judged it and chose winners but declined further programmes because of the demands on his time for making films. News came through that Esmond Knight, a fine actor who had appeared with Stanley in 'The Vicar of Bray' had been made blind in the naval action to sink the Bismark.

In 1943, another Firth Shepherd musical show began at the Saville theatre. It was called *Fine and Dandy* and with Leslie Henson as a home guard and Gavin Gordon as a sergeant. Stanley was a grenadier in a colourful humorous item 'On Guard'. The same trio were joined by Douglas Byng, Dorothy Dickson and Graham Payn for 'Radio Roundup'. It was a parody on the B.B.C. Brains Trust. Stanley was Rear Admiral Camperdown (Not Commander Campbell) and Leslie Henson was Professor Woad (not Joad!).

Stanley was also in his element in *Fine and Dandy* re-enacting George Lashwood, the Lion Comique of Music Hall days, singing "I'm going away". He also sang a song as a tramp made famous by Morney Cash - "I live in Trafalgar Square". The memory of the Great Vance - lived on with Stanley singing "The Motto song - on the square" and the challenge "Cliquot, Cliquot, that's the one for me" to Leybourne's "Champagne Charlie is my name"

In *'Fine and Dandy*, Stanley took the part in a sketch of Claud Spender in 'Fate'. A topical propaganda news item about the Russians defeating the Germans on the Eastern front prompted 'A Story of the Steppes'. The Government home farming Dig for Victory campaign was parodied by Henson, Holloway and Byng in 'Laying for Victory'. The finale was called 'Fools Paradisé and perhaps that is what everyone was obliged to live in. About the show a wartime critic wrote in those very troubled years _ "There is much health in this tonic show: such insouciance has not been lately attained and we are much better for it."

The show ran for 346 performances.

Those too young or too far from theatres were strengthened with a free issue of rose hip syrup and cod liver oil to increase their resistance to head colds and reduce vitamin deficiencies in the plain diet. A scientist named Barnes Wallis was given a free rein to design weapons. His invention of a secret bouncing bomb was one of them. News came through that Guy Gibson and a squadron of Royal Air Force bomber planes had successfully hit and breached the Mohne Dam. The operation to interrupt the water supply to the Rhur armament factories, was thought to be very important and it cheered everyone's morale.

With the Americans coming into the war Stanley was useful for publicity. The idea Our Sam and his musket was easily extended to posters to encourage buying war bonds in the States with Uncle Sam picks up his musket for the war effort.

In 1943, John Barbirolli, whom Stanley had heard at the broadcasting studio, put down his cello bow and raised the baton as conductor of the Halle Orchestra. In the refurbished Free Trade Hall in Manchester, Stanley had seen burning in the blitz, Barbirolli continued the work of founded by Sir Charles Halle in 1858. The nation was comforted and pleased with the broadcasts of music of great composers, either in serious or lighter vein.

CHAPTER ELEVEN

A film Star.

When the Queen's Hall in London was bombed, the famous established Henry Wood Promenade Concerts transferred to the Royal Albert Hall. In June 1944, the allied invasion of Europe began with landings in Normandy, heralding hope for many people. Another more modest but very significant *landing* for the Holloways was that of son Julian into a cot at Watlington, Oxford on 24th June.

A difficult birth was expected and with flying bombs falling on London, somewhere further away than Welbeck Street would be best for mother and child. Laney drove to the hospital at Oxford after Mrs. Crossman, the wife of the Leader of the House of Commons had arranged for her to be attended by the Crossman's doctor. A few days after the delivery Laney drove them home in the little Morris car and Stanley sat beside her *holding the baby!*.

In 1944, Stanley began a very busy time acting in several films. His convincing portrayal of characters, with his very clear diction, made his name a household word for another generation. 'This Happy Breed'. Ten years after speaking those words from Shakespeare at the Palladium, Stanley was chosen by David Lean to be in Noel Coward's film with that title.

PLOT: Set between the two wars, new neighbours Gibbons and Mitchell find they served in the same regiment in 1914. They enjoy the celebrations of peace together, the difficult 1930's and the threat of further conflict.

CAST: Bob Mitchell - Stanley Holloway, Frank Gibbons - Robert Newton, Ethel Gibbons - Celia Johnson who, in writing to her husband Peter Fleming about it, said "Johnnie Mills is playing the son of the man next door. This neighbour is played by Stanley Holloway, a

97

cheerful, full of stories man whom I've always admired".

Patriotic well made British films were popular and made a comforting realistic contrast to the stream of American Westerns and love stories. 'The Way Ahead', a story by Eric Ambler was a film produced by   Two Cities directed by Carol Reed.

PLOT: Men from all walks of life are conscripted into the army. They train together to become efficient soldiers.

CAST: Stanley Holloway - Brewer, Commanding Officer - David Niven, Other ranks - Raymond Huntley, John Laurie, James Donald. Arab innkeeper - Peter Ustinov. Stanley, a cockney and former stoker of boilers at the Houses of Parliament, overhears other conscripts on a train, discussing an M.P. he knew by the nickname of 'Old liver lips'. Stanley tells them he has worked at the House. At the training camp he adopts the role of barrack room lawyer. The members of the platoon, reluctantly thrown together, show their different characters. David Niven had service experience in the war. Peter Ustinov, a true linguist, asked producer Carol Reed, which of the many dialects, did he want him to speak? Reed said "Just make Arabic noises, nobody will know!".

'Champagne Charlie' was made at Ealing Studios in 1944, directed by Alberto Cavalcanti.

PLOT: George Leybourne and Alf Stevens, compete in music hall bars to advertise drinks.

CAST: Tommy Trinder - George Leybourne   Stanley Holloway - Alfred Stevens. Making this film took Stanley back to his boyhood days at the music hall. The Lion Comiques, Champagne Charlie and The Great Vance, are the two main characters who publicise alcohol. They write and sing Victorian drinking songs, much to the dismay of the teetotal movement. Trinder for Champagne and Holloway for Cliquot alternately praise the brand of champagne and every other drink too from gin, ale, burgundy, claret,

98

brandy and Seltzer, port, or rum to sherry wine, trying to boost sales of alcohol.

Stanley was in his element, rolling back the years to his part of Bacchus in the *Co-Optimists*! When the film was released, a critic wrote:-
"Even so, I cannot think how far 'Champagne Charlie' would have got without the controlled flamboyance of Stanley Holloway. Another film critic wrote:-
"Stanley Holloway is in the first flight of British Comedy Actors."

Tommy Trinder   Stanley Holloway
Champagne Charlie   the Great Vance

A useful previous experience for Stanley had been in *Fine and Dandy* playing the part of the *Beau Brummel* of the music halls, George Lashwood. Stanley came on stage as a swell gambler in a frock coat, with top hat and cane. In George Eyton's monologue he pretends to have been to Harrow *College* but is found guilty and transported to Australia.

In 1944 Stanley exchanged some correspondence with Howard Agg, the producer of Light Entertainment for B.B.C. radio. In reply to a request for him to make further programmes of monologues Stanley refused:- "In view of the increasing demands upon my time to make films, reluctantly I cannot not do any more solo recitation programmes and must say goodbye professionally to Sam and Albert". Agg understood but was sorry it ended

Stanley received a golden disc for the record sales about Sam and his musket.

He did appear once that year for the Poetry Society. Betty Driver another popular broadcaster said "It was a pleasure to have known and been in shows with Stanley Holloway". (Betty was a strong *old stager* who appeared up to the 1990's in the Coronation Street T.V. series). A ten year old little girl, Julie Andrews, was allowed to appear on radio with Stanley.

With Germany being attacked on all sides, the end of the war was in sight. Stanley realised the significance of the very sad news of the disappearance of Major Glenn Miller. The famous band leader left on a routine flight to join the American army air corps band in France and was never seen again. He cheered troops and civilians enormously in wartime. Glenn Miller was the first band leader to be awarded a gold disc for the sale of over one million records of "Pardon me boy, is that the Chattanooga Choo Choo?"

Two Cities made a film about Royal Air Force pilots and their families who had to come to terms with the death of their loved ones, just as many people had in the recent real carnage in the skies. *The Way to the Stars* was called *Johnnie in the clouds* in the U.S.A.
PLOT: Friends and relations wait anxiously for the sound of aircraft returning from a bombing mission over Germany. A poetic pilot is lost to his wife and child.
CAST: Michael Redgrave - pilot , Rosamund John - his wife, Basil Radford - duty officer Joyce Carey - harridan hotel resident, Jean Simmonds - her browbeaten companion , Stanley plays the part of a travelling salesman, telling stories badly, giving some light relief.
Anthony Asquith, the Earl of Oxford's son, handled the topical subject very sensitively.
The author and playwright Terence Rattigan, conveyed the same message on the stage at that time with 'Flare Path'. He included the racial problem of marriages to airmen from abroad.

Stanley plays Godby in *Brief Encounter* for Cineguild, directed by David Lean.

PLOT: Housewife at railway station gets some grit in her eye and falls in love with doctor.

CAST: Celia Johnson - Laura Jesson,   Trevor Howard - doctor,

Joyce Carey - Myrtle Bagot, Buffet asst., Stanley Holloway - Albert Godby ticket collector.

The ticket collector at a railway station has some harmless fun, with the buffet assistant.

They provided, as a critic put it, - "Perfectly restrained, flirty banter". Myrtle avoids his

playful grab and says, as a plate of cakes fall. - "Now look, ·   my Banburys are all over the

floor!". Many people thought Celia Johnson had such lovely deep eyes and Trevor Howard

commended on his first part said, he was only a G.P!.(General Practitioner). Joyce Carey had

played several parts for Noel Coward, 'The Master' as he was known in the profession.

Coward chose Stanley Holloway to help provide the complete contrast to the love drama and

insisted the Rachmaninov piano concerto was on the soundtrack. David Lean was not too

happy at first with the comedy element. The film set a stark waiting room had a strong

emotive story and was acclaimed one of the finest of its kind made at that time.

"Brief Encounter"

'Brief Encounter' was filmed at Denham Studios and on location at Carnforth in Lancashire overlooking Morecambe Bay. The Ministry of War Transport gave permission as this was a safe distance away from possible air raids. Floodlights were needed at times and it was made in bitterly cold weather. Noel Coward wrote in his diary -" Saw a rough out of 'Brief Encounter'. Delighted with it. Celia quite wonderful. Trevor Howard fine and obviously a new star. Whole thing beautifully played and directed."

While Stanley was on film sets or relaxing at home in Buckinghamshire enjoying family life with baby son Julian, he could hear the drone of aircraft grouping up overhead at night. There would be news the following day of another 1000 bomber raid destroying the Krupp armament factories at Essen. Hamburg and Berlin were also attacked. Nazi Germany capitulated. The explosion of atomic bombs in Japan at Hiroshima and Nagasaki ended the war in the Far East. There were celebrations similar to the fictional ones in the film- *This Happy Breed*, Then after a General Election, Churchill was replaced as Prime Minister by Clement Attlee.

In the first completely peaceful Christmas for seven years Stanley had a change from film sets. In was at the Casino in London's Old Compton Street as Squire Skinflint in the pantomime *Mother Goose*. He was gleefully booed by the children as the traditional villain they loved to hate. He was supported by comedians Nat Mills and Bobby and Dave and Joe O'Gorman. Roberta Huby was the principal girl and Celia Lipton the principal boy. In spite of clothes rationing in those austere times , Emile Littler arranged gay scenery, costumes and a flying ballet to cheer post war blues. An appropriate Sam monologue by Marriott Edgar mentioned a Christmas pudding becoming a lethal missile in the Spanish peninsula war.

Back at the J.Arthur Rank film studio, a bi-product of flour milling industry,

102

'Caesar and Cleopatra' was planned with director Gabriel Pascal.

PLOT: Bernard Shaw devised the comedy when Caesar was in Alexandria.

CAST: Caesar - Claud Rains, Cleopatra - Vivien Leigh, supported by Stuart Granger,
Jean Simmonds, Cecil Parker, Flora Robson, Basil Sydney, and Kay Kendall.
Stanley auditioned successfully at the Gainsborough Studios for the part of a scornful Greek
soldier - Balzinar. Pascal jokingly told him to stress the word *millers* when he spoke of
Roman trades. It cost over £1 million to make and took two and a half years.
In spite of the star studded cast who braved the English weather in their togas, many critics
and audiences were surprisingly rather bored with the epic end product. Perhaps it would
have have helped everyone considerably to have gone on location in Egypt?

Also in 1946, Stanley was in a film story with an entirely different mood. He was at last
promoted from constable's beat to plain clothes detective Sergeant Sullivan in:-
'Wanted for Murder'. PLOT: a man obsessed by the fact his father is the public hangman.
CAST: Roland Culver - Police Inspector, Derek Farr - suspected man, Dulcie Gray - his
partner. Housekeeper - Kathleen Harrison, added contrasting cockney homely touches.

With Rank again in 'Carnival'. PLOT: An unlikely marriage of a ballet dancer to a
Cornish farmer leads to jealousy and murder by shooting.
CAST: Michael Wilding, Sally Gray, Bernard Miles and Stanley as Raeburn.

The running of the Grand National steeplechase race was resumed at Aintree, Liverpool in
1946. Lovely Cottage was the winner. The Holloways moved home 14 miles from High
Wycombe to a lovely house at Penn called 'Nightingales'. This delightful village west of
London, with pub by the green, was well placed for the film studios and theatres. Stanley had
a largish plot of land and was interested in farming, fascinated by growing crops.

103

The next film Stanley appeared in was for the Gaumont Company. *Meet me at Dawn or The Gay Duellist'*. PLOT: A swashbuckling adventure in which a duel is provoked by a senator and his daughter is unwittingly hired to play the injured party.

CAST: Hazel Court, Basil Sydney, William Eyas and Irene Brown had the leading roles. Director Freedland used Stanley and Margaret Rutherford to add plausibility to the story.

CHAPTER TWELVE

Classic casting.

Ealing studios had built up a reputation for making good films. In 1947, the subject of *'Nicholas Nickleby'* by Charles Dickens was chosen. It gave Stanley a change and chance to work at classical English literature. Producer again, Alberto Cavalcanti, worked with a large cast. PLOT: Ralph Nickleby knows of Nicholas's inheritance entitlement and packs him off to Dotheboys Hall in Yorkshire, where there are no vacations and little diet. The tragedy of the abused Smike is contrasted with the humour of others, including some theatrical players. CAST: Cedric Hardwick, Fay Compton, Bernard Miles, Sally Ann Howes, James Hayter, Derek Bond and Cyril Fletcher make a very talented cast. Stanley played the part of the pompous Vincent Crummels. He provided a contrast to the frightening, evil Wackford Squeers. Crummels has a few good lines to say like "She's the only sylph I ever saw who could stand upon one leg and play a tambourine on the other knee.!". When asked later if he had any preference for a type of character, Stanley said he liked flamboyant people such as ham actors.

Joan Gilbert and Eric Spear were producers of innovative early television shows. Stanley politely declined their invitation to appear because of the demands made on his time for film making. Increasing numbers of black and white television sets were being watched in homes. The popular announcers were Mary Malcolm and McDonald Hobley. Their faces and voices became familiar. When the set was switched on, the B.B.C. caption circled a transmission aerial at Marylebone and a lively signature tune was played. Intervals and temporary loss of broadcasts was covered by scenes of fish swimming in an aquarium, or a potter working at his wheel throwing clay.

From the classic literature of Dickens to some Shakespeare seemed a natural progression. This was the real thing, not like a Co-Ops parody or isolated speech at the Palladium. Laurence Olivier was producing and acting in 'Hamlet'. The actor for the droll gravedigger part was F.J. McCormick but he died suddenly. It was another bit of luck that Stanley was in the right place at the right time. He was asked to step into the part. The young film actress

Jean Simmonds was Ophelia. On location, standing in an open grave in a churchyard, Stanley in thoughtful tones shows Hamlet a skull and asks - "Whose skull do you think this was? This same skull was Yorik's skull, the King's jester".

Olivier, as Hamlet, takes the skull and dramatically replies:-

"Let me see. Alas poor Yorik! - I knew him Horatio.

'O, a pit of clay for to be made For such a guest is meet'

105

The Rank press publicity said of *'Hamlet'* - "'Though a smaller than usual part for Mr. Holloway, it makes up for size by its importance, comically and psychologically. Comedians, since (Gilbert and Sullivan's Jack Point in the *Yeoman of the Guard* in 1888 and *Pagliacci* in Leoncavallo's opera in 1892), have been quite significant rather tragic figures offstage but not so Stanley Holloway, he shows an unsuspected breadth of acting range".

This Arthur Rank film was seen as a milestone in classical dramatic productions. About the director, Stanley said - "Olivier was a strict taskmaster where Shakespeare was concerned. He demanded the best from his actors and tirelessly strives for perfection. Olivier was able to play every part as well as the actor cast for it. This is the most strenuous work of my career".

The world was shocked when radio and newspapers broke the news of Ghandi's assassination. India's Mahatma or Great Soul, (aged 79) had been shot by a Hindu nationalist and silenced at last. Ghandi had been educated in England. He used peaceful methods of civil disobedience, surviving imprisonment in South Africa in 1908 and also by the British in 1931 (when he chose to fast to death). He believed everything must be done to achieve official independence for India. He reluctantly agreed to the partition with Pakistan, as probably the best compromise, in an attempt to end the strife between Hindus and Muslims.

'Variety's the very spice of life that gives it all its flavour' - wrote William Cowper 200 years ago. Stanley's next film role was an exciting dramatic story called *'Snowbound'*. It was made at the Gainsborough studios and on location in Austria.
PLOT: The whereabouts of some nazi gold is sought. Hidden at the end of the war, it is buried in the cellar of an alpine snow covered chalet.

CAST: Stanley plays Joe Wesson, disguised as a photographer, provides opportunities for Dennis Price to search for the bullion. Guy Middleton and Herbert Lom play two suspicious characters who are also searching for the gold. The heroine, Marcel Dalio, knows where it is but keeps her secret. In the search the chalet accidentally catches fire and the *baddies* receive their just deserts.

Through business mergers, the Rank Organisation took control of many British film companies and cinema chains. In 1948 Stanley made *One Night with You*.

PLOT: An English girl, travelling with an Italian tenor is stranded when a train breaks down. There are some criminal forgers also on board. CAST: Guy Middleton, Irene Worth, Bonar Colleno and Stanley as a tramp. Its star was Patricia Roc whom Stanley thought a very attractive lady. A film critic reminded readers that "Stanley Holloway was a broad check Music Hall comedian before he came into films, a jovial jack in the box personality."

Stanley reached the dizzy heights of Police Inspector in the film *Noose*.

PLOT: based on a play about the activities of a gang of black market crooks in Soho. CAST: Nigel Patrick, Carol Landis and Derek Farr. Stanley as Inspector Rendell, investigates their affairs.

If a film studio producer, after the war, was looking for a man to play a scene set on the stage of a Music Hall, who would have been the obvious choice? In the film version of Terence Rattigan's play *The Winslow Boy*, Stanley makes a brief appearance to sing a song.

PLOT: A parent invokes the rights of Magna Carta to have a proper trial, to try to exonerate his son expelled from Dartmouth for allegedly stealing a postal order.

CAST: Sir Robert Norton, Q.C. - Robert Donat. The proud obstinate father, wanting to clear the family name, is played by Cedric Hardwick. Catherine, his daughter, by

107

Margaret Leighton. Solicitor - Basil Radford. The cheerful loyal housekeeper, Violet is played by Kathleen Harrison.

In the story, the family go to a Music Hall. The entertainer, Stanley, seeking audience participation, invites them to call out ideas for extras verses. He has already dealt with topical suffragettes. "What's that sir, the Winslow Boy?! Yes we must have that"
In his element again Stanley sings:- "Just you wait and see why Winslow was treated so shamefully, will they burn their boats at the admiralty? Just you wait and see".
British Lion, London Films, directed by Anthony Asquith had made another dramatic hit.

In his sixth film appearance in 1948 Stanley plays a rich alcoholic, in '*Another Shore*'.
PLOT: A young man dreams of escape to a South Sea island. He is deflected, at the last moment, into marriage.
CAST: Robert Beatty, and Moira Lister. Stanley is monocled Alistair Neil.
Charles Crichton directed this gentle comedy. Nigel Balcon had gathered together around him a strong team and made a reputation for Ealing Studios.

Stanley went on tour in Australia in 1949. He may not have wanted to compete with singer Peter Dawson with his different range and style of recording subjects but Stanley was now making up for lost time in films. T.E.B.- 'Tibby' Clarke kept a flow of skilful scripts coming through at Ealing. In 1949, there were still fenced off partially cleared bombsites awaiting money and rebuilding projects. There was no sign of Stanley's Hotel Pimlico from *A Night Out* in 1920. The cameras went out on location to Pimlico.
PLOT: A shopkeeper discovers of some ancient valuables when he accidentally falls down an old bomb crater. These are identified by a British Museum expert from a crest, as belonging to the Duke of Burgundy. The residents of part of Pimlico hand in their ration

books and want to be treated as foreigners who enjoy duty free goods. The men from the Ministry cannot persuade them to do otherwise. A siege is eased by other Londoners throwing food over the boundary fence of barbed wire. However, misuse of the situation eventually caused a return to normal

CAST: Stanley Holloway - Arthur Pemberton, Barbara Murray - his daughter, British Museum expert - Margaret Rutherford, Ministers - Naughton Wayne and Basil Radford. Supporting cast - Hermione Badderley, Sydney Tafler, and Raymond Huntley.

The probable human reactions to such a situation are very convincingly acted out.

'A Passport to Pimlico' won an academy award for the best screenplay.

Stanley's only other film contract in 1949 was for 'The Perfect Woman'.

PLOT: An eccentric professor makes a robot woman modelled on his daughter. In reply to his advertisement for her to be escorted out, a hard up gent and valet apply for the work. When robot, Olga, is collected for 24 hours, the professor's bored, lonely daughter swaps places with the robot and behaves during the evening out at dinner and in an hotel, pretending to obey the commands Olga responds to. An hilarious story unfolds with housekeeper in a fine cameo part. The reason the professor calls his creation 'The Perfect

Stanley Holloway (right) and Nigel Patrick with Patrica Roc in
"The Perfect Woman" (1947)

Woman' he says is "because she can't talk, can't eat, does exactly what she is told and she can be left switched off under a dust sheet for weeks at a time!''.

CAST: Cavendish - Nigel Patrick, Ramshead his valet - Stanley Holloway, Professor - Miles Malleson, daughter -Patricia Roc, housekeeper -Irene Handl.

Stanley had a well established reputation and the news of Al Jolson's death reminded him of things that had happened since the 'talkies' arrived in 1927. That autumn Stanley took another well earned break and went to Canada. As the 1950 filming season was quieter he was booked to appear briefly in a variety show at the Palace Theatre, Manchester with Jimmy James (who was a past master at acting drunk on the stage). Jimmy's signature tune was "Three o'clock in the morning". It was necessary to be sober and alert to act drunk well.

The only film part in 1950 was in *Midnight Episode'*, a Columbia picture directed by Parry. PLOT: An old busker who stumbles over a dead body finds a lot of money. The CAST: included Wilfred Hyde White, Natasha Parry, Meredith Edwards, Joy Shelton and Stanley played the part of professor Prince.

Stanley was apparently in a film called 'Painter and the post' in 1951 but no details are so far available other than it was based on ' Quinlan's book of comic characters.'

'*One Wild Oat'* had been a very successful farce at the Whitehall Theatre. Coronet/Eros films decided to make their version.

PLOT: A former girlfriend tries to blackmail a solicitor.

CAST: Robertson Hare, Sam Costa, Vera Pearce, Robert Moreton, a young Audrey Hepburn (as a greyhound owner) and Andrew Crawford,(who like Audrey, had an amazingly successful career ahead of him). Stanley as Alfred Gilbey has to dress up as a woman for part of the time. He said it was to fool someone but he was never sure he did. It was a popular film.

CHAPTER THIRTEEN

On the crest of the wave then shipwrecked.

Following the briefest of Shakespeare experiences at the Palladium in 1935 and the very

significant film of *'Hamlet'* in 1948, Stanley's next appearance was again as the gravedigger

but on the stage in collaboration with Alec Guinness in 1951. This was in May for a Festival

of Britain production at the New Theatre in St. Martin's Lane. Stanley enjoyed the part and

Alec presented him with a pewter tankard memento engraved with his line "Go, get me to

Yaughan: fetch me a stoup of liquor". Stanley acted the part of a workman cheerfully,

philosophically singing from the grave as he threw out another shovel full of soil - "A pick-

axe and a spade, a spade, for and a shrouding sheet; O, a pit of clay for to be made for such a

guest to meet".

The next film for Stanley also co starred Alec Guinness. Charles Crichton directed the

Ealing comedy *'The Lavender Hill Mob'* and it proved a unique resounding success. It was

the only film up to that time that was honoured by the Academy.

PLOT: a clerk at the Bank of England supervises the movement of gold bullion. Stanley

owns Jee Jaws,   a foundry making models for the tourist trade. The poorly paid bank

clerk plans a robbery and a gang is formed. The robbery succeeds but the foundry owner,

Stanley, is caught. CAST: Holland - Alec Guinness, Pendlebury - Stanley Holloway,

supporting cast in gang -

Sydney James, Alfie Bass. Waitress- Audrey Hepburn

At the first first suggestion to Pendlebury of the idea of melting the stolen bullion into Eiffel

Tower models he replies "By jove, Holland, it's a good job we are both honest men!"

The temptation is too much and the chance too good to miss.

111

The script writer for for Ealing, Tibby Clarke shows his skill and knowledge. It is very perceptive of Clarke to have Stanley quote at the foundry, Shakespeare's lines from Richard III -

"Slave I have set my life upon a cast".

At the beginning of the film there is a very brief glimpse of a waitress, unknown starlet Audrey Hepburn.

EALING STUDIOS present

Alec Guinness & Stanley Holloway
with *Sidney James & Alfie Bass*

as **THE LAVENDER HILL MOB**

A MICHAEL BALCON PRODUCTION Directed by CHARLES CRICHTON Original screenplay by T.E.B.CLARKE

The men who broke the bank - and lost the cargo!

(whom Stanley was to work with more significantly five years later in another film).

Stanley plays the part of a Broker's man in the 'Festival of Britain' film directed by the Boulting brothers - *'The Magic Box'* which commemorates the British film industry.

PLOT: William Friese Green is trying to perfect the invention of moving pictures.

CAST: Robert Donat - Friese Green, Stanley Holloway - Broker's man, Laurence Olivier - policeman, Joyce Grenfell - lady chorister, and Richard Attenborough etc The Green family run up so many debts that the broker's man has to repossess the furniture.

In the film, Sir Laurence Olivier dons the blue policeman's serge and is the first to see the results of Friese-Green's experiments. Some of these were really carried out Price's studio in Magdalen Street, Norwich.

In 1951 an exhibition site was opened by H.M. the Queen on the south bank of the river Thames. Attractive pavilions were designed and occupied by many countries of the Commonwealth showing off their culture and the quality of products. The site was dominated by futuristic buildings - The Dome of Discovery and Skylon. The Festival Hall was a new venue to commemorate British composers, musicians and orchestras.

At the Festival, special transport arrangements had to be made for the thousands of visitors from all countries. The Holloways, with 7 year old Julian, enjoyed the fine view of the site-seen when walking from Charing Cross, over the Thames Hungerford footbridge beside the Southern railway. Florence Chadwick could have swum across but she chose to conquer the English Channel instead. The Westminster Parliament clock Big Ben on behalf of the State, and the spire and dome of St. Paul's cathedral for the Church, watched silently over the latest innovation in the capital.

Another important cathedral, the blitzed one being rebuilt at Coventry to Basil Spence's design, brought Stanley in contact with the famous legend of Lady Godiva. Earl Leofric of Mercia promised his wife he would reduce the people's taxes if she would ride naked at noon through the streets of the city. Stanley didn't know quite what to expect when Frank Launder invited him in 1951 to be in the film *Lady Godiva Rides Again'*.

PLOT: A shopkeeper's daughter is attracted to the glamour of a beauty competition. Part of the film is set in London among dubious commercial characters.

CAST: Shopkeeper - Stanley Holloway. Promoter - Dennis Price, boyfriend - George Cole, supported by Kay Kendall, Alistair Sim, Diana Dors, Pauline Stroud and starlet Joan Collins.

Censorship was not in fact needed, for the contestants do not have to reveal all.

For the part of the Beauty Queen in the pagent, Frank Launder searched for many months and finally settled upon unknown Pauline Stroud.

In 1952 the bomb site location for *'Happy Family'* was similar to that used in *'Passport to Pimlico'*. On release to the world the film was called 'Mr. Lord says no'. This Ealing film directed by Betty Box starred Stanley as Henry Lord.

PLOT: a shopkeeper is served with a demolition order on his premises to make way for the Festival of Britain. The *house of Lord's* refuses and resists the threat.

CAST: The fine fun characters of Kathleen Harrison, Naughton Wayne, George Cole and Miles Malleson make it a believably amusing story.

From December 1951 to March 1952 Stanley was in South Africa on a trip to the Union in the Commonwealth which helped him to dodge our winter. He was Abanazar again in the pantomime 'Aladdin'. Whilst there he had a telegram from Noel Coward that he was wanted on his return to be in a film *'Meet Me Tonight'*. This was a trilogy of Coward stories directed by Pelissier. Stanley appeared in the one called - *'Fumed Oak'*. PLOT: A down trodden, hen pecked, reliable man, at last walks out of his inhospitable home. CAST: Henry Gow - Stanley Holloway, Mrs. Gow - Dorothy Gordon, their daughter - Betty Ann Davies.

Ealing studios scriptwriter was either clairvoyant or particularly shrewd at seeing ten years into the future. The story of *'The Titfield Thunderbolt'* was a delightful comedy.

PLOT: It is proposed to close down of an unprofitable branch railway line.

CAST: locals, led by John Gregson, Naughton Wayne, Hugh Griffiths and Sydney James, try to keep the service running. Their attempt to have the licence renewed is sabotaged until an engine from the museum saves the day.

114

Stanley's army friend Godfrey Tearle, playing a bishop, bobs up on the footplate stoking the boiler. He shovels coal as a railway enthusiast. Stanley has the part of wealthy retired Mr. Valentine. He is persuaded to invest money on the promise that drinks can be served all day in the bar on a train. Crichton and Ealing scored another hit with this comedy. Ironically fiction became fact ten years later when Doctor Beeching had the task of rationalising the British railways and many small branch lines and stations were closed.

'The Beggar's Opera' by John Gay was made into a film under the skilled direction of Peter Brook. PLOT: A rogue is imprisoned in old London but with ladies help and trickery he escapes. CAST: Laurence Olivier was Macheath and Stanley Lockit the executioner. Supporting cast:- Dorothy Tutin, Hugh Griffiths and Athene Seyler .
Olivier sang himself and later wrote - "Stanley Holloway and I were the only ones using our own voices!". The song they sang,(long before the effects of B.S.E. scare) was -
" In old England our cheer is roast beef and beer!". Stanley thought The Beggar's Opera was one of the most significant films he had been in up to then. He remembered one occasion when he was struggling in a scene to eat meat and gravy whilst singing. Olivier quipped, from their previous collaboration in Hamlet,"I see we have the first gravy digger!". Director Peter Brook said "Stanley knows every trick in the business. When we started the picture he told me how in another film, after doing a scene again and again, Stanley suggested to that director he should look at take two again. He did and it was chosen as the best!".

In 1952 'A Day to Remember' was happy film directed for Gaumont by Thomas.
PLOT: a darts team going to France on a cross channel trip.

CAST: Donald Sinden, James Hayter, Edward Chapman, Harry Fowler and Peter Jones.

Stanley was at the centre of these typically naive English men. Odile Versois provided an

attractive feminine touch with a French flavour. Joan Rice was a starlet who had blossomed

from being a nippy waitress at a Lyons Corner House.

Stanley's experience in pantomime
was useful when he was cast as the
demon king -

'Meet Mr. Lucifer'

PLOT: The arrival and ownership
of television sets subtly showed
the effect it could have on the
few who had one and neighbours
who hadn't.

CAST: Gordon Jackson,
Barbara Murray, Joseph Tomelty,
Humphrey Lestoq, Ian Carmichael,
Kay Kendall, and even brittle
Gilbert Harding appears.

Stanley Holloway stars as a pantomine demon king

Television mania had struck the country with reasonably priced mass produced sets.

Stanley as Sam Hollingsworth is a Jekyll and Hyde character, who brings out the worst in

people The topical story was cleverly written by Arnold Ridley (He was better known acting

the part of Private Godfey in a series about the Home Guard called 'Dad's Army')

Pope Pius XIIth at that time was one of the first to speak out publicly that television was a threat to family life.

Stanley's presence on set was needed for:- *'Fast and Loose'*.

PLOT: the story deals with the situation problems when a married man spends a night at an

hotel and meets a former girlfriend. On stage this it was called - 'Cuckoo in the nest'.

CAST: Stanley - Mr. Crabb works with Brian Reece, Kay Kendall and Reginald Beckwith.

Stanley heard from his helpful *'Sing as we Go'* friend Gracie Fields. She was taking

Capri at her villa Canzone del Mare. She gave a concert for men of the Royal Navy on a ship

of the Mediterranean fleet. Once, after a concert in an aircraft carrier hangar, Gracie said the

captain told them the news. A De-Haviland 'Comet' jet airliner had crashed in the sea after

leaving Rome airport. A search for debris had to be carried out to find evidence of

the cause. Metal fatigue was blamed. This rather justified Nevil Shute's prediction fiction in

the 1948 novel 'No Highway', made into a film with James Stewart and Marlene Dietrich, in

which a new Reindeer aircraft crashes for that reason.

In spite of all the time he spent on sets making films, Stanley said "I prefer theatre to

films. The immediate impact on the audience is so rewarding. You deliver a line and

wham, back comes a laugh, applause or a chuckle".

The B.B.C. did manage to lure Stanley away from film acting on the 4th of July while

Americans were all naturally celebrating. He joined Roy Plomley on 'Desert Island

Discs'. Stanley was castaway number 94. The popular show began in 1942 with Vic Oliver.

Resuming in 1946 after the war, a succession of well over a thousand people have been on it.

Celebrities confide some memories of their life and career. They choose eight records to

take with them and are marooned with a gramophone and inexhaustible supply of needles.

Examples of many of the other famous talented people, whom Stanley knew and worked

117

with, who have also been willingly shipwrecked are :-

Arthur Askey 10, Mabel Constanduros 44, Celia ('Brief Encounter' and 'This Happy Breed')

Johnson 57, Richard Goolden 64 (with Stanley on radio Alice in Wonderland),

Tommy ('Champagne')Trinder 90, Stanley Holloway 94, the man himself!, Leslie Henson

96, (Stanley's mentor), Jack Hulbert 118, Fay Compton 135, Trevor Howard 146,

Nigel Patrick 161, ('Perfect Woman' boss) and ('Pimlico' friends) Margaret Rutherford 168,

and Naughton Wayne 186, Robert Helpmann 190, (Oberon of a Bottom donkey), 'Pukka

Sahib' - Cyril Richard 196, and John ('Titfield') Gregson 253. Anton Dolin, 264, the world

famous ballet dancer said "I appeared in a revue at Blackpool opera house in 1938. The cast

included Elizabeth Welch and Stanley Holloway.

The next time, after the signature tune - "A sleepy lagoon, a tropical moon and two on

an island" had played it was the turn of - Bud Flanagan, 327, Cyril Fletcher,428,

Moira ('Titania, Red Shoes')Shearer, 363, Wilfred Hyde White, 395, Gracie Fields 576,

Stanley Holloway, again! Rescued? 583, Noel Coward 636 (The master), Julie ('Eliza')

Andrews 693, Ian Wallace, 698, Raymond Huntley 867, Alfie Bass 909, Edward Chapman

926, Joyce Grenfell 1074,(another monologuist) Michael Crawford 1080, Robertson Hare

1118, (for the third time and still sowing 'One wild oat') or John Mills 1207.

Such a list of names is almost a roll of honour but they are chosen with one thing in common.

All of these people some contact and significance in Stanley's career and he did perhaps in

theirs. They all accepted Roy Plomley's invitation. A few others may have avoided their fate

by finding some raft of excuse not to come to the microphone.

'Wiv a little bit of luck?' the Dick Richards castaway number 744 in 1965 is the one who

was busy talking to Stanley preparing to write the autobiography up for him.

It would be so good to
hear some excerpts of
these interviews from
B.B.C. archives but how
can they store and
retrieve material from
years and years,
millions of hours
broadcasting before
sophisticated systems
were available?

Arthur Askey said - "Hello playmates!
Stanley Holloway was a lifelong friend"

CHAPTER FOURTEEN

Now acquainted with William Shakespeare and Bernard Shaw.

The Old Vic Company performed 'A Midsummer Night's Dream' by Shakespeare for a
season at the Edinburgh Festival in August, 1954. Stanley was chosen to play Nick Bottom
the weaver. PLOT: Within the play Bottom advises Peter Quince, the producer of the
strolling players, how to run their company. They are rehearsing the lamentable comedy of
'Pyramus and Thisby'. In one brilliant line Bottom suggests the actors meet again and
"rehearse more obscenely and courageously!.

CAST: Queen Titania - Moira Shearer, Oberon - Robert Helpmann, Puck - Anette Crosby,

Helena - Sarah Churchill, Bottom - Stanley Holloway, Flute - Julian Holloway.

Stanley was in his element as the Bottom, the actor who wants to play all the parts.

Stanley's actual talents came to the fore as he demonstrated to his fellows how to play the tyrant, the lover, Thisby with a falsetto voice and a fierce lion. The part of Bottom is a considerable role for anyone to perform but at 64, the donkey's head must have been quite difficult to manage. He has to commune with Moira as Titania. Mendlessohn's incidental dream music provided a wonderful accompaniment to the play and for dances.

The critic of the Stage Magazine said "Titania a breathtaking vision of loveliness, dances with an outstandingly successful Oberon both using flawless techniques. Stanley Holloway is disappointing as Bottom, though his powerful voice is an asset". Stanley thought the show was as prestigious for him as the part of Lockit in 'The Beggar's Opera'. The critic seemed a bit hard on his interpretation of the country bumpkin character. However Stanley was fortunately retained by the company or he would not go have gone on a twelve week coast to coast tour of Canada and the United States and the most significant meeting of his life.

One night at the Metropolitan Opera House in New York, two men watched Stanley acting. Composer and lyricist, Alan Lerner and Fritz Loewe, had been working for some time on a George Bernard Shaw play. Another of Shaw's plays 'Arms and the Man', the playwright had said was "an opera bouffe without music". After very lengthy negotiations with Shaw for permission, it had been transformed into the musical 'The Chocolate Soldier'. The show was first performed in Vienna in 1908 and moved on to New York and London. The show was arranged by Oscar Strauss and Stanislaus Stange. The hit song "My Hero" - "Come come I love you only", also calmed soldiers in First World War trenches.

Lerner and Loewe were rather disappointed that their Scottish musical 'Brigadoon'(1947) wasn't more successful. In the dressing room Stanley was told about the progress with making 'Pygmalion' into a musical - *My Fair Lady*. The 1938 film of 'Pygmalion' had been seen in America with Wendy Hiller and Leslie Howard in the roles of Eliza and Higgins. Anthony Asquith directed a good straight transposition of the story from stage to screen.

Alan had seen Stanley perform in London both in music hall and in the show *Hit the Deck*. Mentioning, on their last meeting in England, the idea of 'My Fair Lady' to Stanley, Alan had strummed over the tune "Get me to the church on time". Now in his New York flat with producer Moss Hart present, Stanley heard the number "Wiv a little bit of luck". Stanley signed a two year contract for the Mark Hellinger Theatre on Broadway in the Spring of 1956. It seemed strange that his career had gone full circle since twenty years previously he had played a policeman in a similar situation with Betty Balfour as a cockney flower seller in Covent Garden.

Back home Stanley was in a film called '*Value for Money*', something he always tried to give though he *didn't appear* to get it this time by making an unusual contribution.
PLOT: A thrifty mill owner's son inherits a wool, shoddy, factory. On an
outing to London,
he meets a night club singer and is infatuated by her. She visits him in Yorkshire intending to marry him but cannot get used to his way of life. She gives way to his girlfriend and marries the other millowner! Stanley doesn't appear on screen at all and his name is not shown anywhere but his is the unmistakable voice of the ghost of Chaley's father. He reminds the son on several occasions not to be extravagant and to consider what things always cost. CAST: Chaley Broadbent played by John Gregson, Susan Stephen - daughter of newspaper owner, Derek Farr - owns another woollen mill and Diana Dors is the dancer,

In December 1955 Stanley arrived back in U.S.A. again to start rehearsal work on *My Fair Lady*. It was planned, when ready in the New Year to have a trial run at Newhaven,

121

Connecticut, fifty miles north west of New York. In a similar way as in England, a show is put on in Manchester or another city before its London run so that cast are very proficient at it and critics can review the production.

Stanley was not called much to rehearsals and in winter and without his wife Laney he felt at a loose end. He phoned up producer Herman Levin three weeks before the show was due to start. As Stanley had done in Chile long ago, he asked if he could be released from his contract. He said the understudy could take over the role of Doolittle. With amazement the request was relayed to impresario Moss Hart. Moss tried to reassure Stanley that his portrayal of Alfred Doolittle was of great importance to the balance of the production. He explained that,in rehearsal, Rex Harrison needed more time to learn sing/speak. (Sprechgesang was an accepted 19 century opera technique for anyone who couldn't sing). Julie Andrews too, needed lots of elocution lessons to be able to cope with the part of Eliza. To play a coarse cockney flower girl and end up speaking like a lady requires much practice.

Stanley was convinced and fortunately he stayed on or he would have missed the greatest opportunity of his lifetime and the one for which he would be most remembered. Moss Hart said Stanley's style and experience with singing and the dance routines were just right for the show.

Before the opening night at New Haven, it was said the revolving stage had a fault. There was more concern that Rex Harrison did not feel he was ready to start. Rex apparently had some difficulties, one of which was relating to the orchestra. The manager, knew that the audience had booked tickets and were travelling up to 150 miles in bitter weather. He threatened to leak the cast and production problems to the Press. During extra rehearsals for Rex, part of one of Stanley's songs was to be cut out. A song, having the prophetic title "Say a prayer for me tonight" was also cut out. (This song of Julie Andrews was not wasted. It was one of the hit tunes later in 'Gigi'.)

However, *My Fair Lady* did open on time at New Haven. The teething troubles were worked out and they moved to the Erlanger Theatre Philadelphia, 70 miles south east of New York, for a month's run for further experience. It preceded the opening on Broadway - on the 15th March, the show began at the Mark Hellinger Theatre. Stanley felt almost immediately the reaction of the audience recognising the brilliant production of a smash hit.

I remember from seeing the show in 1959 and being in a version of it in June 1990, the PLOT: begins, when the curtain goes up, the scene is at Covent Garden fruit and vegetable market in 1912. Stanley, as Alfred Doolittle, is first seen in emerging from a public house, in a tenement section of Tottenham Court Road, wearing his dustman's cap. Sarcastically he thanks the landlord and tells him to "send the bill to Buckingham Palace!". He proudly boasts to his two mates, about the freedom he has given his daughter Eliza, as a flower seller. As her father, Alfie expects to cadge money from her for drink, on the rare occasions they meet. Alfie Doolittle then confides to his pals he is not married to Eliza's stepmother. Eliza appears and gives him a coin with which he goes off singing to buy another drink:-
"The Lord above gave man an arm of iron......with a little bit of luck someone else'll do the blinkin' work!".

In Act 1 scene 4 outside the pub again, Alfie Doolittle learns from the crowd that his daughter Eliza has gone with a swell gentleman to Wimpole Street. She has sent a message arrives from there asking "Please send round my birdcage and fan but no clothes!". Doolittle leaves happily singing again the refrain of "Wiv a little bit of luck", at the prospect of getting some more money out of knowing where she is.

In the next scene Doolittle is ushered into Professor Higgins study. (Dressed in working clothes Stanley has to cough and splutter every night on stage using an irritating wheezy voice.) Doolittle claims to be a member of the undeserving poor. He implies Higgins is taking some advantage from his daughter staying there. He thinks as her father he should share in it. Not knowing why Eliza is there, Doolittle, almost openly sells the favour of his daughter's company. Higgins somehow sees in Alfred's crudeness, an original morality. Henry Higgins gives him the £5 note he asks and writes to a friend in America about the unique dustman.

The main story proceeds with Eliza learning to speak good enough English to be passed off as a lady. Taking her to a ball, Higgins introduces her into polite society and wins his bet with Colonel Pickering. A confused Eliza leaves Wimpole Street and goes back to her old haunts around Covent Garden. She finds her father surprisingly well dressed in top hat and morning suit. An American has left the dustman a lot of money, at the suggestion of Professor Higgins, to found moral reform societies. Also at last her father is going to be remarried.

Stanley as Doolittle leaves the stage carried horizontally, high over his friends heads and sings "I'm gettin' married in the mornin'" The curtain falls with Eliza back with Higgins at Wimpole Street. The four scenes in which Stanley appears are very significant for his experienced acting contrasted

Alfred Doolittle

the differences between the stratas of society. Stanley's rendering of the two rousing brash songs represent the man in the street enjoying the company of his working class. The upper class are seen to socialize by attending ballrooms or watching racing at Royal Ascot.

Some aspects of shows are remembered with mixed feelings by members of casts. Problems can arise and it is interesting to know how they are professionally covered up or dealt with. Michael King played the part of love lorn Freddy Eynsford Hill, infatuated with Eliza. Michael continued to phone Stanley up at Christmas time, long after the show was finished. Michael told Stanley how, when on stage knocking on Eliza's door in Wimpole Street and singing;- "I have often walked down this street before .... knowing I'm on the street where you live", Michael couldn't remember what his stage character name was. In answer to the the maid's question, to which the audience were listening closely, - "Who shall I say wants to see her? he whispered "Who am I?" Not realising why he asked repeated   question, she whispered back- "Michael King!".

At coffee breaks or after dinner speeches, other examples of ingenuity have been revealed. Apparently one night in *My Fair Lady*, a large piece of scenery fell upstage. Rex Harrison carried on unflinching. A bomb scare during the show proved to be a hoax. Other artists remember their *hairy* moments in shows. In a production of the show *Annie Get Your Gun*, the spring trap didn't release the bird, Annie Oakley has just shot with her rifle. A spare was thrown on from the wings and exactly at that moment, the trap belatedly fired. The audience roared their approval when two birds were hit with one shot!. Just like a golfer's rare hole in one. Ian Wallace tells how a hook, used at rehearsal, was not there for the performance and he improvised in front of a curious audience.

Tickets were in great demand in New York and later in London. Stanley remembered how ticket scalpers in the U.S.A. the British call touts, did very well, re-selling them at much higher prices. Tramps, hoboes, bums, which ever name you prefer, slept in overnight queues on the pavement sidewalk and sold their place in the queue for $10 the next morning.

One night in a snow storm the foyer was packed with people hoping to buy cancelled tickets but there were no returns. Stanley noticed an empty seat in the stalls during a performance. The lady holding the ticket reservation said her partner was indisposed. "Couldn't she have given it to another friend?" someone asked. The reply was "It was for my dead husband and all my friends are at his funeral!".

Newspaper critics gave glowing reports of the show. Stanley and Laney with Julie Andrews and Herman Levin attended an after show party at Sardi's arranged by Jules Stein of the Music Corporation of America . When the newspaper arrived they avidly read what the critics had to say. Titles like Hit, Triumph, Spectacular Success, Superb Musical, An All Out Winner, were so pleasing after all their efforts. Kenneth Tynan wrote - "Stanley Holloway is the fruitiest of Doolittles!". Brooks Atkinson wrote in the New York Times - "As Alfred P. Doolittle, the plausible rogue, Stanley Holloway gives a breezy performance that is thoroughly enjoyable". Wayne Robinson wrote in Theatre Arts - "Holloway stopped the show almost nightly with his song and dance numbers". During the show Julie Andrews had her 21st birthday which she shared with Stanley on 1st October, the day he celebrated his 66th birthday. He reminded her of a radio programme they had made together when she was ten.

Rather worrying news came through from Europe about the Suez Canal crisis. A

126

nuclear power station was opened at Calder Hall at the same time and it was thought this new supply might ease future management of fuel resources for heating and lighting..

Stanley received many other invitations to perform. He appeared on the Bell Telephone Hour in a production of Gilbert and Sullivan's *Mikado*. Stanley was Pooh Bah, Lord High Everything Else. Ko-Ko the Lord High Executioner, with his little list of people who would not be missed, was played by Groucho Marx. Stanley thought Groucho took liberties with the script. Once too, rather unkindly Stanley thought, when Helen,(a well built lady playing the part of Katisha), came to rehearsal Groucho was heard to say "Pull up a couple of chairs and sit down". It was all in good fun really. In America Stanley somehow found time to make a recording of cockney songs, entitled - 'Ere's 'Olloway.'

Performing in *My Fair Lady*, Stanley needed to be fit and resilient to survive the strong handling of the chorus at each performance. He is carried out over the heads of chorus every night near the end of the show. He didn't suffer on stage but tripped over a cable extension for an extra fan in his stifling hotel room. With a fractured shoulder, Stanley was very uncomfortable for three weeks. He was well treated at the Leroy hospital. He still made good use of his time. In an enforced break, Stanley made some warm friends in New York among stage colleagues. 'To Stanley Holloway, one of the sweetest, warmest and talented men I have ever known in our beautiful profession - as ever Maurice Chevalier', was a tribute written under a souvenir photograph.

Stanley could afford to spend some time in the sun. On a restful trip to Jamaica Stanley saw Rex Harrison, who was also on leave to marry Kay Kendall. Noel Coward made his house 'Blue Harbour' available to them. Stanley casually said "Thank goodness Julie Andrews and Bob Coote are holding the fort!" At one performance of the show, in the ballroom scene, Moss Hart, who was an experienced actor too, dressed as a gentleman and introduced the lady on his arm to Higgins. The lady was Rex's wife Kay whose unexpected appearance was a typical theatrical surprise!

Up to the 30th September, 1962, performances in New York totalled a record breaking - 2,717. 3.7 million people paid over 15 million dollars (£7 million), to see the show. *Tony* awards were made to Rex Harrison as best actor and Moss Hart as best producer. These awards, named after the American actress Antoinette Perry, who died in 1946, are highly prized by the winners. The sale of records was enormous too. The music was in the charts for 300 weeks and many songs made the number one spot more than once.

My Fair Lady transferred to the Theatre Royal Drury, Lane, London on 30th April 1958 with the original cast and Stanley performed with them for seventeen months up to his 69th birthday. After the opening performance in London, the critic of Theatre World wrote of "Cecil Beaton's fine costumes and the tremendous authenticity of Eliza and Alfred Doolittle". Stanley gave an interview to the Sunday Express casually mentioning some aspects of Rex Harrison's temperament. The printed article was disturbing to Rex, putting him in an unsympathic light. Too much may have been made of some phrases. Stanley was quoted as saying "Rex and I certainly had nothing in common. He never visited my dressing room" Various fragments of other chat were unfortunately printed. Stanley eventually apologised to Rex, saying he had been grossly misquoted and Rex accepted this apology. Rex and Stanley continued to work well together for a year and a half.

In May there were three charity gala performances at weekly intervals for King George's Pension Fund, the Speech and Drama Association and the Royal College of Nursing. At one

128

the Queen Mother asked Stanley if he still did monologues? The Royal Command Performance was on November 3rd with Her Majesty Queen Elizabeth and Prince Philip, the Duke of Edinburgh attending and meeting the cast after the show.

In return for hospitality in the U.S.A., it was not surprising some of Stanley's professional acquaintances at the show and fans called in to see him. Burt Lancaster was in town with his five children and after a matinee they enjoyed theatrical small talk while he signed autographs for them all. Once Stanley looked up in his dressing room from from washing off make-up to see a smiling, teasing - Danny Kaye standing before him.

CHAPTER FIFTEEN

In foreign parts.

Had Stanley wanted to know where the saying 'The world's your oyster' had come from, no doubt his knowledgeable friend Godfrey Tearle could have again obliged by referring Stanley to Act 2 Scene 2 of *The Merry Wives of Windsor*. In the play Pistol is told by Sir John Falstaff - " I will not lend thee a penny". The unusually positive reply at being turned down was "Why then the world's mine oyster, which I with sword will open"

Although many more people are now travelling, not everybody has or will go abroad. Those who take a package holiday have a different experience from anyone going to live and work overseas. Travel as well as broadening the mind brings memories of interesting sights. Other considerations may have been coping with the weather, sleeping, signs, labels and words in another language. The food and accommodation may differ considerably and in some places English may not always be understood or spoken fluently. The management of currency, travellers' cheques and passports (and their security during local outings), are other significant factors. To go to work abroad however, to entertain, perform, fulfil a contract and communicate with a non English audience, adds another dimension.

As a young man, Stanley had crossed Europe by train to live in Italy for a few months to have singing lessons at Milan in 1914. Then he went by mailboat to tour to Brazil and Chile in South America with the Grotesques concert party, crossing Caruso's path en route..

Stanley hadn't much choice about organising entertainment in the trenches in 1915 but his peacetime appearance abroad had been very limited. He did go briefly to Paris with the 'Co-Optimists' for a very short season. It would be   difficult to assess the reaction of the French to British humour. Opera in a foreign language is one thing that is somehow international. Subtle cultural jokes must be difficult to convey clearly in another tongue. Subtitles under films provide an immediate translation but the quick point of a joke would be lost. In 1927, as able seaman Bill with in *Hit the Deck*, Stanley sang as lustily as anyone - "Join the Navy and see the world". Being in entertainment in the theatre and cinema could prove to be as good a passport. It was being films which opened the door to world travel.

In 1933 Stanley flew to Paris for some location shots in *The girl from Maxim's*. He was also employed to make some commercial radio appearances in Paris for Philco,
He said flying the 250 miles from Croydon to Le Bourget in a silver Handley Page Hengist and Horsa biplane,took about three hours and was quite a precarious adventure. When his friend Pierre de Caillaux, music director at the Paris Rex cinema came over to London ,
Stanley returned hospitality by arranging a low flying treat for him. They flew from Heston near the present Heathrow airport and the charter pilot was a former backstage boy of the Co-Optimists. The hair raising flight close to Windsor Castle upset Stanley's stomach.

In 1933 too,Stanley had an unusual invitation to go to Canada. He was invited to speak in

Toronto to the immigrant Society of Lancashire Men. The nett fee of £1,000 for the short engagement in North America, with travel and hotel accommodation expenses paid, was a considerable sum at that time. Few other stars could command such a fee.

A 'Stray Saying' of George Bernard Shaw's was - "Every man over forty is a scoundrel". This would not apply to Stanley aged 43, though he would have spent much time away from Queenie and the four children. That year he clocked up much overseas mileage and would have been rated as one of the most travelled people in show business.

For his first visit to America, Stanley accepted an invitation from Cliff Whitely, Co-Ops director friend and now an impresario. With Jack and Claud Hulbert and Bobby Howes in the party Stanley passed the Statue of Liberty, sailing up the Hudson River into New York harbour. When he saw the skyscrapers on the Manhattan horizon, he was sharing a sight achieved by many immigrants from European countries, (and hoped for by many more.) Cliff Whitely's party checked in to their reservations at the Waldorf Astoria hotel. A friend of Stanley's, Alan J. Lerner, who had seen him perform in *Hit the Deck*, asked Stanley to look him up and "Sing Hallellujah" again, if ever he was in the States.

New York is known now as the *big apple* but it wasn't quite as ripe in 1933, struggling to shrug off the effects of the depression. Stanley could see some similarities with the busy streets of London where he was born. His first impression was of an artist at the Paradise Club singing "Did you ever see a dream walking?". Stanley was certainly in something of a dream but it was more of a nightmare. New York, to him, never seemed to close down for a couple of hours and let him get some sleep. In London peace at least reigned every night for a few hours, without air conditioning or double glazing to muffle the noise.

Before 1939 and much more afterwards, with improved transport, more people travelled

131

in all directions. Musical stage shows and artists moved to North America from Europe and the return process grew. Entertainers from the United Kingdom were exported on tours to the Dominions of Canada, South Africa, Australia and New Zealand, to which many British people had emigrated.

In 1949 Stanley went on tour to Australia. Five year old son Julian and Laney went too, for the cruise on the Orcades. At the end of March, the Sydney Morning Herald had a photo of the family on board, leaving London for a six month tour of stage and radio in Australia and New Zealand. Under the management of David Martin, Stanley had his own show with the Tivoli Circuit and was on stage twice nightly at the Theatre Royal, Sydney.

He also appeared at Tivoli when they moved, nearly a thousand miles further south, to Melbourne. He was billed, with Sam's Waterloo cap on, as 'The Renowned Comedy Star of Stage, Screen, Radio and Records'. Through the media of the last three, he was well known to Australian listeners and viewers. The Sam and Albert monologues and his range of songs had gone *down under* before him. Produced by Ralton James, the show was advertised as 'The biggest international all- star cast of the year'. It included muscular movers - The Romanoff dancing trio from Europe. The U.S.A. was represented by dancers Grace and Nicco and Rolly Rolls from Radio City New York. Ben Wrigley with Joy Dexter and Dick Thorpe were an amusing group from England. They appeared twice in each half before Stanley with accompanist Billy Mayerl topped the bill at the end of the second half and joined in the grand finale.

An article in the Morning Herald on 23rd April, the day after the Holloways docked in Sydney, was headed-" Star Comedian bans 'Blue' jokes". Stanley was quoted as saying "The only public a comedian could build up to last a lifetime comprised the family unit and relatives. If you deal with the 'blue' you don't cater for them". The reporter went on to say Mr Holloway has a new number 'Albert Down Under' dealing with Albert's adventures with a lion he met on the voyage out! The reporter was told Stanley was now devoting himself almost exclusively to films and would probably play the part of Long John Silver in a Disney's production of Treasure Island. (Time proved that Stanley's co-star friend in *This Happy Breed*, Robert Newton, was actually given the peg-leg part.)

It was also very interesting to read in Sydney Morning Herald on 23rd April,1949, a heading close to the report on Stanley's arrival. Another caption - 'Mr. Holloway's Defence', the Acting Prime Minister, Mr. Holloway, bearing the same name as Stanley, disagreed with a statement to the Sydney Chamber of Commerce by Mr.A.E. Heath their president, (not either Ted, P.M. or bandleader of U.K.!), that, "The 40 hour week was a national mistake!." Mr. Holloway said "The principle of a 40 hour week as the basis for a week's pay was quite economically and socially sound. Many manufacturers had adopted it prior to the Court's approval. History has proved that such reductions have eventually been a blessing to all the parties in industry".

When the show moved on to New Zealand, at his hotel in Wellington in North Island, Stanley was introduced to a Mr. Brown. He was the mysterious investor, living the other side of the world, who helped start the successful Co-Optimists run in England in 1920's. He was very pleased with the big profit dividends had brought him. Stanley made films again on his return to the United Kingdom, then in the autumn went to Canada.

At the end of the Festival year 1951, with the experience 'Hamlet' on stage behind him and many people enjoying the film - *The Lavender Hill Mob*, Stanley took a working winter break. He sailed on the Union Castle mail ship from Southampton to Cape Town to

133

the Union of South Africa. On the Blue train to Johannesburg he had the misfortune to have terrible toothache and his face swelled up. From a station, producer Frank Rogaly telephoned ahead and on arrival at the Carlton Hotel, a dentist and doctor were waiting to treat him. During a pleasant three months in South Africa, Stanley did all the usual things in his leisure time. There were plenty of fresh Outspan oranges to eat and he was taken to see gold mines. Native labourers in their break time dressed up in Zulu costumes and impressed him with a demonstration of their traditional dancing. During a visit to a diamond mine at Kimberley, news came through that King George VI had died. Stanley performed in the South African capital Pretoria to white European audiences who appreciated the art of pantomime. On returning to Cape Town, a telegram from Noel Coward about a film caused Stanley to use the release clause in his contract, allowing him to hurry home.

Young son Julian had also been on the tour and Stanley tried to book a flight stopping over in Rome on the way back. Fortunately, Stanley could not get reservations and read in the newspapers that the connecting flight from Rome, they would have caught, had crashed at Frankfurt. The disaster however, did not deter him from flying.

Having made 'Fumed Oak', in England, part of the film for Noel Coward, in 1953 Stanley and Laney flew off to Canada. The 6,000 mile round trip was simply to appear on television for six minutes. Shirley Maclaine, the American film star who Stanley met briefly once on a set remarked about travelling around so much in theatrical work, "I want to go on living out of a suitcase for the rest of my life. I'd love it, if I had a fifty-foot by thirty-foot suitcase!"

In September the next year Stanley returned to North America with The Old Vic company for a twelve weeks tour of Canada and the United States as Bottom in 'A Midsummer Night's Dream'. Son Julian now ten years old had the part of Master Flute, the bellows mender.

In 1955, December was not the best month to go alone to New York when most people aged 65 were relaxing with money collected from their deserved pension. Stanley was to commence rehearsals of *My Fair Lady*. He was based at the Algonquin hotel in an even busier, noisier city than he had discovered twenty years before. Though there were facilities open for 24 hours, Stanley said he would "swap it for rural Buckinghamshire, any day!" He liked the skyline and occasional outings. It became boring walking around Central Park on snow covered slushy paths or watching T.V. on the wide choice of channels. Popcorn doughnuts and ice cream sodas are mostly for the young. After he had asked to be released from contract to return home, the theatrical management made more efforts to see he had friends and was entertained in company to which he was accustomed. Sid Fields amused and was photographed with him. Dean Martin invited Stanley to appear on his T.V. show.

In 1960 there was a still a demand for a lively veteran performer and Stanley went back to New York in the Fall for a one man show at the Ethel Barrymore Theatre.

CHAPTER SIXTEEN
Cinema scope.

The film must go on as well as the show. Even with *Mv fair Lady* in full swing at Drury Lane, Stanley had the energy and made the time for other things as well. In 1958, a film *'Hello London'* was made and Stanley sang two songs in it - "Petticoat Lane" and "Sing a song of London".

At the Royal Variety Show at the Coliseum on 3rd November, great artists from the Good Old Days, came rather like arrangements for the Cavalcade of Variety which Stanley compered in 1935. This time G.H. Elliot age 75 sang his most famous song still sighing

135

"By the light of the silvery moon". Miss Hetty King maintained that "All the nice girls love a sailor". Max Bygraves introduced the younger stars - Norman Wisdom, Harry Worth, Eartha Kit, Harry Secombe, David Nixon and Charlie Drake. Stanley aged 68 might have been with the Good Old Days contingent but he was very much still in harness and needed in the finale of excerpts from *My Fair Lady.*

Somehow Stanley was temporarily whisked away to island locations and studio to make *'Alive and Kicking'.* PLOT: Three ladies escape from a Home and renovate a hut on a tiny Irish island. They pose as nieces of a millionaire. MacDonagh visits the island which he has inherited. He helps the ladies organise a wool knitting industry.
CAST: Stanley - MacDonagh, ladies - Sybil Thorndike, Kathleen Harrison and Joyce Carey. It was well directed by Cyril Frankel, an ex army entertainments officer.

In between the *Midsummer Night's Dream and My Fair Lady* years Stanley played parts in a couple more films. Eye catching titles are important. *'An Alligator named Daisy"* certainly did just that. PLOT: deals with complications of having a young alligator in an ordinary home. A songwriter is confronted with such a problem. Reptiles have big appetites and can grow as big as 3 metres or 10 feet long!
The CAST: Donald Sindon, James Robertson Justice, Margaret Rutherford
Roland Culver, Frankie Howard, Jimmy Edwards, Diana Dors & brittle Gilbert Harding try to handle the problem in an hilarious way.
Producer Thompson promotes Stanley to the part of a senior officer.

From this small part Stanley next co-starred in a comedy with Frankie Howard directed by Carstairs called *'Jumping for Joy.'* PLOT: Jack Montague has to take care of a very different animal, a greyhound!. The story moves between living in a disused railway

136

carriage to attending dog tracks at race meetings, until some gamblers are outwitted and exposed. CAST: Stanley Holloway - Jack Montague, Frankie Howerd - his friend, A .E. Matthews - a delightful eccentric old gentleman, Joan Hickson, Alfie Bass and Lionel Jeffries.

In 1959 Stanley played the part of Kipper, a bookmaker, in a film shown in black and white called - 'No Trees in the Street'. Ted Willis wrote the PLOT: The theme was love on the dole in a family living in the slums of London in the 1930's. There was conflict over the honest or illegal earnings of a deprived family. CAST: Herbert Lom and Sylvia Sims play the main characters. Stanley in a pub, sings about winkles - "Picking all the big ones out".

Reflecting other highlights over these years, Stanley remembered seeing with family and friends some of the procession of great musical shows passing through London theatres. Oklahoma by Rogers and Hammerstein had been at Drury Lane exactly ten years before My Fair Lady. "A bright golden haze on the meadow" proved as valuable here as for the 2,212 shows in America. Irving Berlin competed in his way with Annie Get Your Gun at the Coliseum. Perhaps it was history repeating itself that, just as D'Oyly Carte had sent Oscar Wild to America in 1881 to prepare American audiences for Patience, so the wartime friendly supporting invasion of G.I. servicemen had prepared us for recent U.S.A. history. Stories of migration westwards opening up land use in new states was interesting.

Carousel in June 1950, also at Drury Lane, captured the summer mood of fairgrounds. It was another romantic and dramatic story by Rogers and Hammerstein. The stream of brilliant shows and stories was followed by South Pacific at Drury Lane to warm our winter. Perhaps these very successful escapist shows helped civilians and servicemen "wash right out of their hair" the unhappy experiences in the previous ten years in Europe and the Far

137

East. Stanley once said "earlier British audiences really loved well delivered sad songs." When as a young artist, after he had sung "When we go down the Vale" a little flippantly, he was advised never to make fun of a serious song in the wrong circumstances..

Stanley left the cast of *My Fair Lady* at Drury Lane on 3rd October 1959, two days after his 69th birthday. His friend, colleague and understudy James Hayter assumed the role of Alfred Doolittle. Pre-publicity before the New York and London openings suggested the show had much to offer and this certainly proved to be right.. Drew Middleton, in describing Stanley's London performances, said "he seemed a bigger,more impressive figure". R.E.P. Sesenfelder of Philadelphia wrote that "of the many productions of Pygmalion, Holloway's was the best Alfred Doolittle I have ever seen". The residents of both cities took to their hearts the characters in the romantic rags to riches story. Americans were particularly amused by "Why can't the English learn to speak? Stanley found out that Robert Coote as Colonel Pickering was the son of a Co-Optimist colleague.

When I went to Drury Lane, Alec Clunes had replaced Rex Harrison and Tonia Lee took over the Julie Andrews Eliza role. Stanley was still very much in evidence as Alfie and I age 26, as a mature college student, was very impressed indeed with his part and personality. I carefully kept my programme which cost 1/- (5p) It bore a picture of Charles II. Looking now at what was advertised then shows some interesting changes. Extended play recordings of the show cost 11/6d (57p). A Jaeger coat cost £10.52p. A Morphy-Richards vacuum cleaner with super suction was £25 and North Thames gas cookers could be bought from £20. Kingsway cigarettes were 4/- (20p.) for 20. Bear Brand *'fair lady'* wondrous nylon stockings with tapered heel cost 9/- a pair.(45p).

Increasingly, the countries of the post war world accepted American financial aid.

138

Fictionally in *Call Me Madam*, Lichtenburg refuses the offer. Ambassador, Sally Adams, found one country that wished to be self supporting. "It's an old fashioned idea marrying for love" was a symptomatic musical statement about the changing values of society. When Stanley was playing at theatres run by Oswald Stoll, his attention was drawn to a notice in dressing rooms which said - "Artists are requested not to ask for free seats. If their friends can't pay to see them how can you expect the public to?!".

Julian Holloway arriving home from Harrow for the Christmas vacation and New Year celebrations, said "I was kind of knocked out to hear father had to report to Buckingham Palace on 24th February." In going to the Palace for an investiture Stanley did not know quite what to expect. Someone else described their impressions - 'We walked across the palace forecourt, climbed flights of crimson carpeted stairs on between ranks of smart household cavalry. In a waiting room an under secretary steward sorted out the various ranks of investiture from M.B.E. to Knight. At the end of a grand corridor hung with portraits of kings and queens, the Ball Room itself had six huge crystal chandeliers, two royal thrones and a military quartet.

Did Stanley hear "Get me to the church on time" being played as he received his Order of the British Empire? It was presented to him by H. R. H. The Duke of Edinburgh. Her Majesty was indisposed. His Royal Highness said "They're playing your song again." Stanley proudly rejoined his family Laney and Julian, smiling happily.

Many famous men and women have collected an award as tribute to their skill and the profession. Harry Lauder rose from the Music Halls and stepped up to kneel and be knighted by King George V in 1919 as "I love a lassie" echoed down the hall. William Gilbert knighted at last in 1907 by King Edward VII, belatedly fifteen years after Arthur Sullivan's

139

accolade from Queen Victoria. Savoyards music was playing at the time - 'The soldiers of the queen' from *Patience*. For Gracie Fields - "Sally" naturally, was being played in 1938 when she received a C.B.E. from King George VI and in February 1979, when she was made a Dame Commander of the British Empire by Her Majesty Queen Elizabeth II.

American audiences were still hoping for the return of Doolittle in some shape or form. In October Stanley went back to New York for his one man show 'Laughs and other events' for a week at the Ethel Barrymore theatre. The critics wrote- "it was a flop because it was too frail as Broadway entertainment". It hadn't the instant impact they expected. Recordings of Noel Coward in Las Vegas showed he knew the American public's taste. Some of his well known songs were therefore delivered at a slightly quicker tempo in a catchier way.

From America, Stanley sent a message to the B.B.C. to Eamonn Andrews for the 'This is your Life' programme. Harry S. Pepper of Co-Optimist days, had risen to be an important producer for B.B.C. Stanley was unexpectedly chosen for a reunion on the air, to share memories of his career. The B.B.C. kept trying to pin Stanley down for another programme and managed to interview him on Woman's Hour. Also in the musical adaptation of Dickens 'Oliver Twist'. Stanley's voice was well suited to the new role of Fagin singing "You've got to pick a pocket or two!".

It was enough for him to undertake one film per year. In 1961 'No love for Johnnie' was filmed in new cinemascope for a wider narrower screen. and directed by Thomas.
The PLOT: was about political problems of a Labour Member of Parliament.
The CAST: led by Peter Finch included - Donald Pleasance, Billie Whitelaw, Hugh Burden, Rosalie Crutchley, Dennis Price, Fenella Fielding and Stanley as Fred Andrews.

On Sunday evening 24th July 1960, having made a new Long Playing 33 record with PYE,

Stanley was back on the air in the B.B.C. Home service from 9.15 to 10p.m. in - 'Frankly Speaking. This chat show was presented by John Freeman and Philip Hope Wallis. They encouraged Stanley to talk about his career and travels. Following his enormous success *My Fair Lady*, the elder statesman of entertainment, told them how active he still was in the theatrical profession. He was very willing to talk to them about the busy life of a gentleman with the *"Arm of iron"*. He was in another show 'Meet Mr. Holloway'. It was arranged by Harry Carlisle, with the popular George Mitchell singers joining in choruses. Transatlantic travel now was frequent and Stanley appeared on Canadian pay television in Toronto with an old friend Gracie Fields. Street publicity was done for them by means of a large double decker bus. It drove around the city displaying their names, in large chocolate coloured letters.

'*On the fiddle*' was a new experience for Stanley in 1961 with a film again directed by Frankel. PLOT: For a wartime butcher's shop owner, an Aircraftsman spiv, purloins some carcases of meat from the camp kitchens and makes the butcher' daughter pregnant. Father has to somehow to manage the good and unwelcome extras.
CAST: Mr Cooksley - Stanley Holloway, sharp aircraftsman - Alfred Lynch, Kathleen Harrison, John le Mesurier, Eleanor Summerfield and Eric Barker. Experienced actors and actresses cannot possibly guess which newcomers they work with will succeed in the profession. In this film, another airman character nicknamed Gypsy is played by Sean Connery! Some film apprentices certainly blossom out into mega stars!

Stanley travelled back to the U.S.A. in the autumn or fall of 1961. He was booked to be on a series for A.B.C. television sponsored by Pontiac Motors and the American Tobacco Corporation. It was called 'Our man Higgins' (not Doolittle!. There is no connection for

141

Higgins is the perfect butler inherited by the MacRoberts family). They must retain him to keep the rare and valuable silver dinner cutlery service. The story was based on a radio programme It's Higgins, Sir''. The T.V. show ran for thirty four episodes. from 3rd Oct. 1962 to 11th Sept. 1963. Stanley's son Julian, studying at R.A.D.A. the Royal Academy of Dramatic Art, also appeared in the show as nephew Quentin Peabody Polewhistle.

The Higgins programme gave some light relief to anxious families whose fathers and sons were serving for U.S.A. in the war in Viet-Nam. News of communist Russia's success in orbiting the earth with cosmonaut Yuri Gagarin in a sputnik was slightly worrying but John Glenn soon showed the worth of the American astronauts.

There is an old music hall song "I'm following in father's footsteps, I'm following my dear old dad". George Formby did this when his father died prematurely from the damage to his lungs, received when working near furnaces. Dad left the foundry to become an entertainer. Formby Senior wanted young George to benefit from his factory experience and have an outdoor job. George Junior was apprenticed to a riding stable in Eire, to train to be a jockey. George junior however returned to show business after his father died. He made a fine career in films and the theatre.

Sons or daughters of famous fathers and mothers may find careers difficult to choose. What will they do with their lives? Sir Peter Scott was the son of the Antarctic explorer. Scott junior made his own way as a wildlife conservationist and artist. The offspring of some notabilities may naturally seek low key anonymity. Others continue to search for fame such as Donald Campbell who, after his father's death, also became the fastest man by 1966, travelling on land or water.

Stewart Knowles interviewed Julian Holloway before a programme - The Man from Haven.

Julian when age 9 nine played the washerwoman in 'Toad of Toad Hall' at his prep school.

He went to Harrow and enjoyed cricket. His father hoped perhaps that the initials J.R.S.,

Julian Robert Holloway would look good in cricket score books. Julian might even play for

England. They enjoyed playing batting and bowling together in the garden at Penn.

In view of all the time he spent as a youngster in the wings at theatres or film sets it

was not too surprising that after Harrow, where Julian played Bottom the weaver in A

Midsummer Night's Dream, 6 years after he had seen his father perform the part with the

Old Vic. Although the Daily Telegraph reporter made a favourable comment, Stanley

seemed to find it difficult to give praise on the spot. Julian read in Stanley's autobiography

'Wiv a little bit of luck' that his father thought he was good in 'When did you last see your

mother?'. Stanley perhaps found it difficult to accept that his son began his career acting a

serious part of a homosexual, like public reaction to Noel Coward's avant garde play

about drug addiction 'The Vortex'. Julian went on to perform in several humorous *Carry On*

films and carved out his own style of acting and directing in the theatre.

The B.B.C. announced Stanley Holloway would be the guest on Desert Island Discs on

12th February, 1962. Most listeners didn't know Stanley had been marooned ten years

previously and chosen his eight records. Otherwise it would rather shatter the illusion if he

had been rescued.

Many Americans were still stunned at the assassination of President John F. Kennedy

in Dallas on the 22nd November. The Great Train Robbery of £2.6 million in England was

insignificantly by comparison. What the much younger Harold Wilson would do

remained to be seen.

CHAPTER SEVENTEEN

The icing on the cake.

1964 was yet another very busy and significant year for Stanley. In America he appeared with The Fantasticks - the Hallmark of Fame, a very important television programme. It brought him back into contact with a comedian, Bert Lahr, whom he had previously met in 1933 on a visit to the States. They went our by taxi to Brooklyn and did a sketch together called 'The Vegetable Song' about rearing children being better than gardening. James Stewart visited Stanley's dressing room. Stanley returned the praising drawl "Good show!" with memories of Stewart's fine film performances especially in *No Highway'*, about planes and metal fatigue and also *'The Glenn Miller Story'* tribute to the 'Moonlight Serenade man'.

Stanley returned to Philadelphia where *My Fair Lady* really took off at the Erlanger Theatre. He was booked to perform at Forrest in four performances of "Cool Off". In Sheridan Morley's - *Great Stars*, Stanley played the part of Lester Lindstrom a cop.

It was proposed to make a film version of *'My Fair Lady'*. Several successful stage musicals have been made into films. The casts are occasionally the same but often different names may be introduced which are better known to cinema audiences and improve takings at the box office. One such example from *'South Pacific'* is the part of Nellie Forbush, played on stage by Mary Martin and in the film studio by Mitzi Gaynor. Also Ethel Merman (who couldn't apparently be "as quick on the trigger" for cash) was replaced by Betty Hutton in the film *'Annie get your gun'*.

Jack Warner, head of Warner Brothers Studio in Hollywood, who had already employed Stanley in films, before, bought the screen rights of *'My Fair Lady'* for a record 5½ million dollars (£2 million). With the cost of scenery, locations, stars and back up a massive investment was being made. It was vital to cast the right people to insure success and a good profit. The director George Cuckor set about choosing the right balance of characters. Unlike a stage show, in filming there may be many *'takes'* and place settings are not always shot in a logical or chronological order. Because of this the actor has to use different techniques to ensure a smooth performance in the running of the complete film. Such film techniques expose stars to more close up facial shots seen much more clearly on the screen than stage.

Although Julie Andrews had been very good indeed as Eliza in theatres, Audrey Hepburn dearly wanted the part. Early in her career she had met Stanley when appearing as a receptionist in *'One Wild Oat'* in 1951 and as briefly as waitress Conchita in *'The Lavender Hill Mob'*. She was chosen for Eliza and was paid $1million. Julie was given the advice 'when one door closes another opens'. (She went on to win an Academy award the next year, for her portrayal of *'Mary Poppins'* and later for Maria in *'The Sound of Music'*). Later in her book Audrey Hepburn said "*'My Fair Lady'* is the most exasperating film I've been in". After working very hard at the skills required, she was crushed to learn Marni Nixon's singing voice would be dubbed on to the film. It was during a rehearsal that producer Cuckor broke to the cast the news - "J.F.K.'s been shot!.The President's gone" but they went on working.

Rex Harrison had had plenty of film experience with *'Major Barbara'* and *'Blithe Spirit'* but Warner doubted his name as box office attraction in America. Other names were seriously considered for the part of Professor Henry Higgins. Noel Coward was asked. Michael Redgrave, George Sanders, Jose Ferrer and even Rock Hudson were very possible but Cary Grant was the studio favourite. Although a Londoner, he did not see himself in the part and so Rex Harrison was offered it. Robert Coote as Pickering was almost unknown.

145

Wilfred Hyde White was given this part as he frequently appeared as a film character. Stanley had worked on sets with him before in *'Midnight Episode'* for Columbia in 1950. Jack Warner and Cuckor thought James Cagney, with his song and dance experience, (though he was not as well known in Europe for this as his gangster roles), would probably be better for Alfred Doolittle. He was much younger than Stanley who was 74. Alan Lerner possibly had a casting vote on this. Stanley was asked to be Alfred Doolittle again but the father to a different Eliza. Jeremy Brett took over from Dennis King the role of Freddy Eynsford- Hill.The rest of the cast worked on the filming until June, whereas Stanley's part didn't take very long.

At the Royal Command film performance in 1958, at the London Coliseum on 3rd November, it was the turn of a few of the first Drury Lane stage cast and new film members to shake hands with Her Majesty the Queen. Rex Harrison ironically, when you think of all the actors considered before choosing him, did win the Tony award! Julie Andrews was among the celebrities present. Though it was Audrey Hepburn's night of celebration, Rex graciously said he would divide the trophy between his two fair ladies.

Of Stanley as Alfred Doolittle a critic wrote - "As Eliza's dustman father, Stanley Holloway was demonstrating the manner and mien of a brewery horse kicking up its heels in spring time". When Stanley was asked to comment on his world wide acclaim he said "I've grown accustomed to the pace!" He was often asked to compare the performance of Julie and Audrey but he said he couldn't squeeze a cigarette paper between their skills.

The big screen version in technicolour attracted millions of people to see it all over the world. Jack Warner's gamble and expertise paid off handsomely. "Dad is so ridiculously young" said son Julian at an interview. When is enough enough? Aged 75 Stanley was

146

asked to be Blore in a film of Agatha Christie's mysterious murder story - *"Ten Little Indians"*. The location was a disused mansion in Rush near Dublin. In the very cold March weather it was not as pleasant as experience of making *The Vicar of Bray* 30 years before. CAST: Stanley's friend Wilfred Hyde White was joined by Leo Genn and Shirley Eaton. To improve marketing of the film in countries where English is spoken, Hugh O'Brian (Wyatt Earp a film cowboy marshall) was invited along *for the ride* together with American Pop singer Fabian. Israeli star Dahlia Lavi, tried to insure some cinema seats would be filled in Mediterranean countries. Stanley and all the cast survived the weather, not actually dying off in turn as in the plot.

Were Stanley's globe trotting days over? In 1965, with four young men called 'Beatles' collecting their M.B.E's at Buckingham Palace, Stanley took up an invitation to film in Hawaii. Otto Preminger directed *'In Harm's Way'* for Paramount Studios and Stanley was still a box office attraction. The CAST: included other senior film stars - John Wayne, Larry Hagman, Kirk Douglas, Franchot Tone, Patricia Neal, Henry Fonda, Dana Andrews, George Kennedy, and Hugh O'Brian, again!.

They assembled to make a movie about the retaliation of the United States Navy and Army Air Corps to the attack on Pearl Harbour. Stanley played the part of Clayton Carfil, an Australian planter, similar to the role of Emile de Bec in 'South Pacific'. With blackened face Stanley was paddled in a dinghy and shinned up a palm tree to spy and signal information to guide his troops through enemy lines. Working in such heat on location when you are 75 can take some of the pleasure out of balmy sandy shores and warm blue seas. To be filmed climbing a palm tree on to a leafy hut roof is a tall order at any age. Endless supplies of refreshing pineapple were available. When he returned home, actor and elder

147

statesman of the cinema Stanley, had his eardrums checked over by his doctor.

Stanley had been near some very loud broadside salvos fired from an offshore warship.

In Hollywood staying at the Beverly Hills hotel one day a taxi driver, realising his fare was British, asked what he thought of the area. Stanley told him he liked California because it was a nice warm place. The driver sarcastically added, because of the state of their atmosphere at that time - "It's the one place in the world where you wake up to the sound of the birds coughing!". Much has been done now in cities to deal with smog.

In 1966, the incorrigible Stanley was still performing. A film 'The Sandwich Man' was made with Wilfred Hyde White, (yet again!). Michael Bentine is the star of the PLOT: Walking around around London streets daily with his advertising sandwich boards, he meets many characters. Stanley bobs up in a flower bed in a park. Other fine CAST: include- Dora Bryan, Norman Wisdom, Harry S. Corbett (of 'Steptoe' fame), Diana Dors, Donald Wolfit and Frank Finlay. Stanley said it It was great fun making the film. When first released it was spurned but after Goon Shows and Monty Python genre had educated the public to other forms of humour, it was more acceptable later on television.

In March 1967, Stanley had a wish come true. He said if he was ever down on his luck he would like to be a butler. He enjoyed being a fictional valet in 'The Perfect Woman' in 1949. and guarding the silver on American television in 1961 as 'Our Man Higgins'. B.B.C. television producer Michael Mills was making his version of 'Blandings Castle'. The CAST: was Ralph Richardson as Lord Emsworth, the 9th Earl needed a butler. Stanley as Beach, his butler, pants at his Lord's beck and call, complaining about his feet, the stairs and serving trays. In the Radio Times Stanley said, from his own castle, Nightingales at Penn in Buckinghamshire, "I could see Windsor Castle from my window - 'if it wasn't for the

trees in between'. A popular Music Hall song Stanley's contemporaries knew uses the words
- "If it wasn't fur the 'ouses in between". The band of the Coldstream Guards playing the
background music for this film was conducted by Ron Grainer.

Journalist Dick Richards had a considerable knowledge of entertainment in theatre and
films. He wrote a book called 'The Curtain Rises'. In 1966 he spent much time talking over
and taking notes about Stanley's career. The book called 'Wiv a little bit of luck' - The life
story of Stanley Holloway was published by Leslie Frewin and was on sale in bookshops in
1967. The conversational style showed a talented 75 year old reminiscing about all the
interesting people and events and mostly about show business. The book proved popular and
a second impression was made.

The world about him was speeding up when Stanley was beginning to gear down. Some
amazing things had happened during the sixty years since sinking of the Titanic. Stanley had
experienced many ups and downs in shows and films until the grand finale as Doolittle. He
once said, although enjoying the Shakespearean parts, he didn't want to end up in *King Lear!*

On 21st July 1969 the 11th Apollo space mission successfully landed astronauts Neil
Armstrong and Edwin Aldrin on the moon. Almost weightless they hopped about fulfilling a
dream prophesy of President Kennedy. W.S. Gilbert had Hilarion sing "They intend to send a
wire to the moon, very soon", in *Princess Ida* in 1884, at the end of the Savoyard era.
With the Armstrong first step for man, the prospect of George Orwell's '1984', drew ever
nearer. The supersonic airliner, the Anglo-French Concorde has proved safe and viable so
anyone could buy a ticket and travel faster than the speed of sound. What should Stanley
aged 80, occasionally taking slow drives in his Rolls Royce, make of all this?

Stanley was still in demand to play characters in small cameo parts. In *'Mrs. Brown you've got a lovely daughter'* Stanley plays the part of George George Brown.

The name arose apparently because his father stuttered at the christening service!

(Others know of a girl really being christened - Anne *Withany* Jones, at the font,

because the vicar asked the parents how to spell Ann!)

PLOT: a grocer's wife in Covent Garden (that place again!), has a greyhound (the daughter)

around which the story revolves.

Other CAST: are Mona Washbourne in the tile role, Peter Moon and Herman's Hermits

feature in this. Nat Jackley sings "My old man's a dustman". It made Stanley feel at home in

the cockney atmosphere. Produced by Saul Swimmer, Ron Goodwin provided the music .

A film 'Run a crooked mile' that year was for transmission on colour television.

PLOT: A man suffering from amnesia stumbles accidentally upon a secret and is then

manipulated by some businessman for their advantage.

CAST: Louis Jourdan, Mary Tyler Moore, Wilfred Hyde White (When is he not involved?)

Stanley Holloway, Alexander Knox and Laurence Naismith.

'How to make it' or *'Target Harry'* in 1969 was a film with PLOT: about various criminals

trying to discover the whereabouts of printing plates for bank notes that had gone missing

from the Royal Mint. The cast included Vic Morrow, Susanne Plechette, Caesar Romero and

Charlotte Rampling and Stanley. Directed by Henry Neil and produced by Sharon Compton

Then Stanley went to Canada to play the part of Burgess in G.B. Shaw's *Candida*. This was

at the festival   at Niagara on the Lake. Shaw's words first heard in 1898 - "We have no

more right to consume happiness without producing it than to consume wealth without

producing it", seemed good advice now,to people and politicians. However Shaw with other

comments like 'I am a millionaire. That is my religion' and 'There are two tragedies in life - '

150

One is not to get your heart's desire, the other is to get it!' made his contribution, that continued the 'play within a play' syndrome of Shakespeare. The very perceptive philosophy of American Frank Waldo Emmerson also attempted to persuade people to evaluate and reason about Life themselves and all the influences affecting them.

For October 1st 1970, Julian Holloway organised a surprise eightieth birthday party for his father at the Savoy Hotel. One can imagine Stanley with Julian, greeting show business friends who just happened to be there. One of these was Sir Alec Guinness. He had appeared with Stanley in the film 'The Lavender Hill Mob', twenty years previously. I wrote to Sir Alec in February 1989 at the Comedy Theatre where he was performing. He kindly replied saying "Stanley Holloway was a delightful, cheerful and kind man. The last time I saw him was at a private lunch for his 70th birthday. Stanley didn't know it was me, he thought he was lunching alone with his son. We happened to go into the Savoy together and kept spotting old friends. (The lunch had been kept a secret and he greeted them with "Fancy seeing you here!"). Not until we got into the dining room did the *penny drop* that it was a lunch in his honour. He was knocked sideways by it but very delighted." One can easily imagine the similarity with the This is Your Life programme. In this case, no doubt when the doors were closed and glasses filled, everyone was upstanding to wish and toast a surprised Stanley "Good health " and "Happy Birthday to you" was inevitably sung.

In the interview with Stewart Knowles, Julian told how well he got on with his father now - "The funny thing is the man's a freak. So ridiculously young - I have never thought of him as an old man. He never seemed old to me and he began to seem even younger than he did when I was a kid".

151

CHAPTER EIGHTEEN

Such a lot of living.

Stanley in 1970, had a small part as a gravedigger again but this was in a comedy film called '*The Private Life of Sherlock Holmes*'. In the CAST and PLOT: Colin Blakely as Doctor Watson reveals some cases from an old manuscript in which Sherlock Holmes, played by Robert Stephens, unusually becomes involved with women. This Billy Wilder effort included Christopher Lee, Clive Revill and Catherine Lacey. The critic said "a very pleasing civilised entertainment, affectionately conceived and flawlessly executed.

A more important film in 1971 for Stanley was '*Flight of the Doves*'. It was produced for Columbia/Rainbow and directed by Ralph Nelson. It was based on the novel by W. Macken. PLOT: two children run away from their bullying stepfather to join Irish grandma. CAST: Ron Moody, Dorothy Maguire, Stanley Holloway and Willie Rushton.

In 1971 on the 18th December, there was a memorial service to the great British actress Dame Gladys Cooper. Stanley read from John Bunyan ('The Pilgrims Progress'). Celia Johnson read a sonnet from Shakespeare and Ian Wallace sang.

In 1972, '*Up the front*' was a comedy. The PLOT is that a footman is hypnotised into enlisting for the army in World War 1. The fun centres around the fact he has an enemy plan tattooed on his bottom!
The CAST included Frankie Howard, Zsa Zsa Gabor, Bill Fraser, Hermione Badderley, Lance Percival and Stanley Holloway reunited with Robert Coote, (Pickering on Broadway.)

Naturally the elder statesman of stage and screen did not take on too much now. He gave various interviews. He said "The variety artist, more than any other, depends on his wits and presence of mind. He recalled how an audience helped him without realising it.

Also his moustache mascot, used in recitations as Sam, sometimes became partly detached from his nose. Once he had to finish the words with his head tilted backwards to avoid losing it altogether, and this caused more laughter. It was nearly lost completely once and only retrieved from a waste bin just before the performance.

Reminiscing about his time at Birmingham at the Hippodrome, he had invited the audience to join in "Wiv her head tucked underneath her arm". To avoid unnecessary embarrassment in a family show, he got them to sing Blackpool instead of Bloody Tower. The correspondent of the Birmingham Mail wrote - "As a character comedian Stanley Holloway has few equals. Albert is confined to bed. The doctor orders the medicine to be taken in a recumbent posture. The Ramsbottom family rush around local shops to buy one!"

Stanley appeared on a television chat show and was interviewed by Michael Parkinson. The experienced compere put famous people at their ease in front of the cameras and had some excellent replies to his promptings. They discussed monologues and how Albert came to be disgorged by the lion. Apparently Stanley said there had been complaints to the National Society for the Prevention of Cruelty to Children. These to N.S.P.C.C. were followed by some from the Animal Rights Protection Society! They laughed at how serious some people are. It was like Noel Coward being pilloried for his fun song "Don't Let's be beastly to the Germans".

On stage at the Cambridge Theatre in 1972 a critic thought playwright David Ambrose with 'Siege' had taken on a very difficult task. PLOT: Present and past Prime ministers are advised by a steward. CAST of only three - Michael Bryant as Prime Minister, Alistair Sim as the former party leader and Stanley Holloway as Sigwick, the club head steward (like butlering again!). The steward stars putting *the man in the street's* viewpoint clearly to the politicians. Robert Waterhouse reported in Plays and Players magazine 'Stanley Holloway devotees, flocking to see him up West since *My Fair Lady* will be very disappointed by the very few minutes he is on stage'. It reminded Stanley of the reception of *The Three Sisters* when the audience booed because Dorothy Dickson had too small a part to play.

Stanley, as a guest at the Houses of Parliament when a member can invite his constituents along to see where he works, was greeted by various M.P's. In talking to him, some began to recite their favourite monologue. Stanley went to H.M.S. King Alfred when invited by Peter Scott to entertain cadets. It reminded him of the film *'The Winslow Boy'*.

In 1973 Stanley returned to the Shaw Festival In Canada. Her Majesty Queen Elizabeth and Prince Philip attended the gala performance. Stanley remembered there were 23,000 in the audience and it was difficult to project a voice to the back of the amphitheatre.
The Watergate scandal was a main item of world news in 1974. and in 1975, from boring into the North Seabed, gas began to flow supplying the United Kingdom .

Still a cinema box office attraction, Stanley appeared in *'Journey into Fear'* in 1976. PLOT: a munitions expert is threatened in Istanbul by assassins. CAST: Shelly Winters and Vincent Price were the stars. This was a remake of an Orson Wells 1942 film, little seen.

In 1977 Stanley then 87 toured Australia with Douglas Fairbanks Jnr. aged 88! The show was called *The pleasure of his company.* They performed at the Comedy Theatre Melbourne from Monday 25th April. Supporting CAST: David Langton, Carol Raye, Vince Martin, David Goddard and Christine Amor. It is difficult to envisage what they did and for how long, for audiences attracted by their famous names.

Stanley received a special award from the Variety Club of Great Britain -
"For his contributions to show business during his long and distinguished career".

Stanley read from the book of Ecclesiastes in the Bible on 'Stars on Sunday'.

He chose the words from the plaque that had hung on his bedroom wall for so long. The philosophy of King David's son still seemed to make some sense today. "What do we show at the end of our life of labour? Fast runners do not always win the race. Listen to the quiet wise man rather than the shout of fools. There is a time for every purpose under heaven".

The philosophy Joyce Grenfell adopted seemed to apply to Stanley,who admired her performance. She said "I don't believe in luck. I do believe in recognising opportunities, being open to them and then having a go. I felt from the very beginning things were going to work out alright". Although Stanley enjoyed singing "Wiv a little bit of luck" they were Lerner and Loewe's words, Stanley had reached New York in 1956 after many years of making the most of any opportunity that occurred.

One possible piece of luck he didn't enjoy was believing an old couple who told him they had left him £200,000 in their will. They died 18 months later with no fortune. He wondered what difference a win on the pools (or now, national lottery) would have made to his life. It is a situation cleverly expressed in the film 'Laughter in Paradise' in which Stanley was not involved. Hugh Griffith plays the part of an eccentric man who dies. In his will he says relatives must perform embarrassing duties to qualify for a share of the inheritance. The CAST: Alistair Sim must commit a robbery, Fay Compton must work as a housemaid and George Cole, a timid bank clerk, must rob a bank but fumbles when sticking up his own and becomes a hero. Fulfilling obligations in a humorous way, they find there is no money.

One of Stanley's film producers, Henry Cornelius of 'A Passport to Pimlico' in 1949, said "He has a sharp sense of character coming from working in ever changing variety programmes. Whilst portraying people with gusto,he makes the characters profoundly real."

155

Peter Brook said of the 63 years old Stanley, when directing the film of 'The Beggars Opera' - "He seems to grasp the situation in a flash". Summarising the film work in his book British Film Character Actors, Terence Pettigrew wrote "Stanley Holloway played a long catalogue of warm, human characters, predominantly comedies but some serious roles". Stanley said "Ordinary verbal jokes don't interest me as much as creating a scene in which the audience can see the situation with you. Nobody will laugh if you tell them you fell off your bike. Take the audience into your confidence and describe the ridiculous spectacle of another person falling off a bike and you have created an unthreatening picture they can share." Someone else said "He is a good mirthmaker because he has that English trait of being able to laugh at himself". Authority Eric Midwinter said Critic Sir Harold Hobson agreed that Stanley Holloway's expansive personality relaxed and pleased audiences of all kinds. He evoked in them 'a maelstrom of uncomplicated happiness'. Working a lot with his Yorkshire dialect, Stanley had also been known to recite a Sam Small monologue in French with a good accent. He had picked it up on various visits to France. He thought non cockney artists, playing a film part needing that tongue, were mostly fairly obvious phoney attempts.

Musically Stanley said "I taught myself to play the piano by trying out chords and finding which were harmonious". In an interview with Nick Brown, Stanley said- "Whilst I had never had any idea of going into opera seriously, in one way I wish I had. To sing pieces especially written by the great masters and perhaps appear at La Scala Milan or Covent Garden would have been so good".

Stanley told how he admired the stagecraft of others. The soft shoe shuffle dance and voice of Eugene Stratton with "She's my lady love" was included. He enjoyed Lottie Collins colourful vivacious personality, with clear diction in "Ta ra da boom de ay!"

156

The timing and delivery of comedian Rob Wilton's words was an example to everyone - "The day war broke out, my missus says to me, what are You going to do about it?!" Billy Williams in a velvet suit sang "I must go home tonight" and Stanley enjoyed singing that song too. Stanley said "I mourn the departure of the Lord Chamberlain and censorship. I think we are all children in show business, a lot of us, anyway. You need to be kept in order. It helps to know what should and should not be allowed to be performed"

Confiding to interviewers about himself, Stanley said he liked to be very punctual. Son Julian said for his wedding to Zena Walker - "He and my mother were there terribly early, of course, then they always used to get everywhere about an hour early. We got married at 12 and they were there at 11 - at least three marriages before ours - and they had to kill time walking round the block." That song "Get me to the church on time" keeps cropping up!. Julian said "I'm one of the few people who have always remembered to put O.B.E. on letters to him and his letters are signed O.B.E. and O.A.P. I like to think of my father getting into the Rolls Royce and going to draw his old-age pension, a few months at a time,having paid in for it all these years". Stanley said later "I arranged to have it sent for the older you get,the more insurance you have to pay on your car and I am very old!".

Living in "dear old Sussex by the sea" as the county anthem goes, he was well thought of locally. His neighbour Robert Nesbitt asked Stanley to do something for Sir Noel Coward's birthday celebration. Stanley joked about the reverence of the acting profession, 'The Master' as Coward was known, saying "It must be holy week!" With much feeling and , appropriately for a great all round artist who qualified by birth , Stanley sang - "London Pride has been handed down to us" which Noel was inspired to write in London when another Liza's Covent Garden coster barrow was avoiding the falling bombs.

157

Stanley's ideas of relaxation were enjoying an occasional swim in warm water, an infrequent round of golf, a glass of champagne and water - separately! He sang to make money and live but he was always wanting to appear before an audience. Just as Sir Noel Coward said his reason for living abroad was simply - "Tax", when I spoke to the late Donald Adams, after performing in chorus with him at Great Yarmouth, I asked why he could perform in an indifferent television Savoyard production? He replied honestly - "Money!". Everyone has to live and if they have a famous name, others will obviously be making much more money from their appearance. Stanley admitted to being thrifty whilst others were over generous. There are plenty of examples of former stars who unwisely wasted away much of their incomes and ended in poverty.

Stanley said his favourite poem was Rudyard Kipling's 'IF'. The late actor Robert Morely also loved to recite this. The poem written a hundred years ago under the title "Brother Square Toes - Rewards and fairies", won the vote for the nation's favourite poem, in a recent poetry competition for radio listeners. Kipling succinctly touches upon many aspects of life, and most people, if they are honest, can identify with at least one of the sentiments.

Locally in retirement Stanley officially opened the Oxfam charity shop in Bayford Road, Littlehampton on 1st August, 1977. The editor of the local newspaper, Brian Shewry said as a guest at a school in 1979, when pupils staged their version of *My Fair Lady,* Stanley admitted it was the first time he had actually watched a production of the show. Also in his review Mr Shewry said, that when Stanley was not well enough to start a sponsored swim at St. Margaret's School, Angmering, he sent along a tape recorded message. Mr Holloway was president of the Young People's Light Orchestra since formation in 1974. Peter Nightingale, the conductor, said "Stanley liked to be kept up to date with our activities.

We sent him a copy of our Christmas carol tape and he wrote a letter of thanks. When in good health he visited our rehearsals from time to time".

In November, 1980 when he walked on to the stage of the Palladium, a comment in the Sunday Times in Birthdays of the Week said "Stanley Holloway 90 - unique charm endured for over 50 years". He motored up to London to be in the Royal Variety Show. Happily he appeared with old friends and colleagues - Arthur Askey and Cyril Fletcher ('Alice in Wonderland' on the B.B.C.), Tommy Trinder ('*Champagne Charlie'* to Stanley's Vance), Arthur English, Chesney Allen (whom Stanley had worked with as Ches sang with Bud Flanagan "Underneath the arches"), Richard Murdoch, Sandy Powell, Ben Warris, and Billy Dainty. Stanley shuffled round in front of a full house with television cameras turning. Carefully rehearsed, with their hands on the shoulder of the one in front, the fine veterans appropriately sang the great Flanagan and Allen favourite - "Strolling". The steps were planned for Stanley to end up near the microphone for him to announce the next artist - Paul Squire, who sang the 1964 Neil Simon song "On the other side of the track", from *Little Me*. Roy Hudd, dressed to impersonate Max Miller, led Stanley back to his dressing room.

When asked how a ninety year old spent his time in retirement he said "Pottering - which means putting on a kettle and taking it off again". He had long managed to live with attacks of asthma. His eyes became affected by glaucoma. He said "I can't read any more but do bits of crosswords. I listen to Crosby, Sinatra or Tchaikovsky records". Like a Samson, an obstacle free route in his garden enabled him to continue to take steps and a breath of ozone. He said "I've had the other life, the parties and the fuss. Now I am happy to hear the birds singing and it's peaceful". Stanley had taken an active understanding interest in Voice of Progress, the taped newspaper for the blind, directed by Nicholas Hare.

159

With his wife Laney, he attended five balls at Goodwood organised to raise funds for V o P.

Stanley said in his book he liked to sit back sometimes by the fire and reflect -

"what might have happened if I hadn't taken a film role at Twickenham?

I might never have met my present wife, Laney. My life would have been so much poorer.

Supposing Leslie Henson hadn't visited his mother at the Essex seaside, that far off summer?

Where would my career have led. Supposing Gracie Fields had not persuaded me to take a

bash at variety? A whole phase of my career wouldn't have happened."

In January 1982 Stanley Holloway was admitted to the Nightingale Nursing Home in

Beach Road, Littlehampton as he had had a slight stroke. He died eleven days later on the

30th and is buried in the churchyard at East Preston. The **'Arm of Iron'** was tired out. Father

time, whom Stanley had often seen on the wind vane at Lord's, whilst watching cricket said

"Out", Not quite a century but what a very memorable innings!. His name was in the

Guinness Book of Records as the oldest entertainer.

In the summer of 1989, I was busily researching Stanley's life as an example of our

Theatrical Heritage. I drove through London to Wentworth Road, Manor Park, and took a

photograph. A neighbourhood watch person asked if they could help me. When I mentioned

my purpose they offered a damaged sign of the Avenue which had been replaced. At All

Saints Church in Romford Road I saw the proudly hung framed picture of choirboy, master

Stanley. Moving on to the Theatre Museum at Covent Garden I saw that the stage props

donated - cap, boots and drum were well cared for. Driving down to Sussex, where I was not

expected, Mrs. Holloway kindly agreed to talk to me the next morning. When I left with

helpful notes and ideas buzzing through my mind, I called in at the little cemetery.

The headstone reads - *In EVER LOVING MEMORY of Stanley Holloway O.B.E. Actor*

1st October 1890   30th January 1982   Adored Husband of "Laney".

I looked down at the fresh primulas and also saw I was, by pure chance, wearing brown

suede boots! - "I ask you, who'd have thought have going in Brahn boots?."

I felt very happy and very grateful for all the memories Stanley Holloway had bequeathed us.

In the obituary in The Times, under the title 'Rumbustious Cockney actor and singer'

it said Mr. Stanley Holloway, O.B.E. may have made cockneyism internationally popular.

His was an unforgettable presence whether on stage or screen. The local newspaper in

Sussex comments were entitled 'Stanley - Doolittle who did so much!' They summed up for

this nation people's lasting impressions of him.

If you have access to Internet and feed in the name Stanley Holloway, the words of

Albert and the Lion, Albert's Return, Runcorn Ferry and Albert's Reunion are printed out.

No credit was given to authors, publishers or recorder, it merely said 'From the

Stanley Holloway record'. I sent the information to the publishers of his monologues. Perhaps

this is another technological phase in storing material, which everyone can use now and

benefit from. Increasing use of Internet could perhaps at least mean people in the next

millenium will see the name Stanley Holloway and ask questions about him. I hope for their

sake and any other researchers in the near future, this book will be useful.

Stanley once said he wished he had collected the fee for Voice Over advertisements on

television. I looked up from my set when a familiar voice said "Try pulling one lid over the

other one". He was there again with Joyce Carey in the background, advising Celia Johnson

what to do about the grit in her eye. The clip from the film *'Brief Encounter'* just before

doctor Trevor Howard takes over, was being used for advertising insurance.

A Sunday newspaper colour supplement listed what lots of famous people left in their wills. The amount beside Stanley's name was £94,000. Quite modest by today's celebrity standards.

In the 1990 B.B.C. programme *Pull Out the Stopper'* which I instigated and helped provide information, we heard Mrs. Holloway talking to Ian Wallace. She showed him old programmes of the boy soprano at Chelsea and predictions by phrenologist. Excerpts of early sound recordings of the Co-Optimists were played. Guests Sir Alec Guinness referred to Stanley's thorough approach to his work when they made 'Lavender Hill Mob'. One cross moment arose when their counting preparation was not considered work. Sir Michael Marshall talked about discussions he had with Stanley over the complete books of monologues published in 1979. Julie Andrews remembered some anxieties Stanley had in America with Moss Hart over rehearsals of *My Fair Lady.*

The Radio Times advertisement of the show on 2nd October, 1990 said "Stanley Holloway will be affectionately remembered for his ebullient performance of Alfred Doolittle in the stage and screen musical." Producer Nick Clarke's script and sound effects were very good. George Hoare, Manager of the Theatre Royal recalled the first memorable night of the show in London. Anne Rogers, who understudied Julie Andrews in the role of Eliza, remembered meeting Stanley in Central Park. They looked at squirrels roaming freely.

When I heard the broadcast of 'Pull out the Stopper', I was quite surprised the recorded extracts showed so clearly the hacking cough that dustman Doolittle inflicted on Henry Higgins every night! Also the cheeky rich laugh preceding "I'm gettin married in the mornin". It was also good to hear from archives some words Stanley, as Pooh Bah, exchanged with Groucho Marx in the televised *Mikado.* A perfect finale was for me to hear for the first time the words of a song from his second show in 1920 - *A Night Out*

"It'll be all the same, all the same a hundred years from now,

No use a worrying no use a hurrying no use kicking up a row

For I won't be here and you won't be here when a hundred years have gone

For somebody else will be well in the cart and the world will still go on".

The radio critic Gillian Reynolds praised the work of producer Nick Clarke

and presenter Ian Wallace.

When I looked at my copy of Shakespeare to check the words Stanley spoke to *Hamlet*

as the gravedigger I noticed the advice Polonius gave to Laertes:-

" but do not dull thy palm with entertainment."

Thank goodness Stanley took Gracie Field's advice and not Shakespeare's.

School in the old days was about the three R's - Reading, wRiting and aRithmetic.

Were Stanley's three R's - Recitation, Rendering songs and Reacting characters on stage?

Stanley thought Kipling's 'IF' significant: he met with triumph and disaster and treated those

two imposters just the same as, for 92 years he seemed to fill the unforgiving minute.

The theatre owes much gratitude to the man with the Arm of Iron, Stanley Holloway.

My heartfelt thanks are offered to Stanley for and on behalf of anyone who has enjoyed

finding out with me as much as they could about what he so generously gave us.

In the local town market square, an electronic traction engine organ from the Cushing

collection at Thursford was playing. My ears picked out the delightful churning of

Let's all go down the Strand", and "Burlington Bertie" still "Rising at 10.30!

We have a truly great theatrical Heritage to draw upon.

Appendix 'A'

<u>Monologues Performed by Stanley Holloway.</u>

Title   - first line   Author   Date

AND YET I DON'T KNOW   Weston and Lee
Now, my sister's daughter Elizabeth May   1919

OLD BARTY   Douglas Grant
If you want to travel for miles round 'ere   1919

MY WORD YOU DO LOOK QUEER   Weston and Lee
I've been very poorly but now I feel prime,   1923

OLD SAM   Stanley Holloway
It occurred on the evening before Waterloo,   1929

'ALT WHO GOES THERE?   Stanley Holloway
Old Sam First came to London when George IVth were King 1930

BEAT THE RETREAT ON THY DRUM   Weston & Lee
I'm hundred and two today, bagoom!   1931

ONE EACH APIECE ALL ROUND   Stanley Holloway
No 2468 Private Samuel Small were up before his captain 1931

THE LION AND ALBERT   Marriott Edgar
There's a famous seaside place called Blackpool   1932

THREE HA'PENCE A FOOT   Marriott Edgar
I'll tell you an old fashioned story that Grandfather   1932

SAM'S MEDAL   Mabel Constanduros & Michael Hogan
You've heard of Samuel Small per'aps?   1933

RUNCORN FERRY   Marriott Edgar
On the banks of the Mersey, over on Cheshire side   1933

OLD SAM'S PARTY   Mabel Constanduros
Sam Small, though approaching his eightieth year   1933

MANY HAPPY RETURNS   Archie de Bear
Down at the school house at Runcorn,   1933

GUNNER JOE   Marriott Edgar
I'll tell you a seafaring story,   1933

THE RETURN OF ALBERT   Marriott Edgar
You've 'eard ow young Albert Ramsbottom in the Zoo   1934

MARKSMAN SAM   Marriott Edgar
When Sam Small joined the regiment,   1934

WITH HER HEAD TUCKED UNDERNEATH HER ARM W.& L.
In the Tower of London, large as life   1934

THE BEEFEATER   Weston and Lee
Oh dear, another day I suppose   1934

SAM DRUMMED OUT   Weston and Lee
When a lad's been drummed out of the Army,   1935

ST. GEORGE AND THE DRAGON   Weston and Lee
Some folks'll boast about their family trees   1935

SAM'S STURGEON   Ashley Sterne
Sam Small were fishing in canal   1935

THE JUBILEE SOV'RIN   Marriott Edgar
On Jubilee Day the Ramsbottoms asked all their relations 1937

ALBERT AND THE 'EADSMAN   Marriott Edgar
On young Albert Ramsbottom's birthday   1937

THE 'OLE THE ARK   Marriott Edgar
One evening at dusk as Noah stood on his Ark   1937

SAM'S FORTUNE   Stanley Holloway
It happened one evening in Wigan, (Austin car advt.)   1938

JONAH AND THE GRAMPUS   Marriott Edgar
I'll tell you the story a really remarkable tale   1937

OLD SAM'S CHRISTMAS PUDDING   Marriott Edgar
It was Christmas Day in the trenches in Spain   1939

THE RECUMBENT POSTURE   Marriott Edgar
The day after Christmas, Young Albert   1939

ALBERT EVACUATED   Stanley Holloway
Have you heard how young Albert Ramsbottom was evacuated 1940

PUKKA SAHIB   Reginald Purdell
The Green eye of the little Yellow God by Milton Hayes   1940

SAM GOES TO IT   Marriott Edgar
Sam Small had retired from the army   1941

HE GEORGE LASHWOOD MONOLOGUE   Frank Eyton
I've always been a gambler since the day when I was born 1942

ALBERT'S SAVINGS
                    Stanley Holloway   1943

ALBERT DOWN UNDER   Stanley Holloway
Adventure with lion on the voyage to Australia.   1949

SWEENEY TODD, THE BARBER   Weston and Lee
In Fleet Street that's in London town   1957

THE BATTLE OF HASTINGS   Marriott Edgar
I'll tell of the battle of Hastings as happened   1975

THE MAGNA CHARTER   Marriott Edgar
I'll tell of the Magna Charter as were signed   1975

THE PARSON OF PUDDLE   Greatrex Newman
In the clean little, green little, God-save-the-Queen   1975

ALBERT'S REUNION   Stanley Holloway
You've heard of Albert Ramsbottom and Mrs. Ramsbottom   1978

There are three monologues Stanley Holloway recited
that were written earlier in the 1900's:-

ON STRIKE   Charles Pond   1906
When I lays dahn my tools I lays 'em dahn

EVINGS' DORG 'OSPITAL   Charles Pond   1906
'Ere, Evings wasn't always in the dorg trade

THE STREET WATCHMAN'S STORY   Charles J. Winter   1910
Some chaps gets the fat and some chaps gets the lean

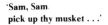

'Sam, Sam
pick up thy musket . . .'

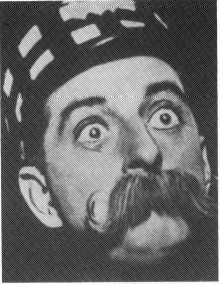

Films in which Stanley Holloway appeared.

Year	Title	part	page number
1921	The Rotters	Arthur Wait	71
1930	The Co-Optimists	himself	72
1932	Sleeping Car	Francois	72
1932	The girls from Maxims	Mougincourt	72
1934	Lily of Killarney (Bride of the Lake)	Father O'Flynn	72
	Love at second sight (Girl Thief)	policeman	73
	Sing as we go.	policeman	73
	Road House.	Donavon	74
1935	D'ye Ken John Peel (Captain Moonlight	Sam Small	74
	In Town Tonight	himself	75
	Squibs	P.C. Lee	75
	Play up the band, Sam's medals) 'Alt! who goes there,) Beat the retreat. Cartoons) Sam and his musket. 1½d a foot)	Sam Small	75
1937	Song of the Forge	Joe Barrett	76
	Village Blacksmith		
	Vicar of Bray	Vicar	76
	Cotton Queen (Crying out loud)	Sam Owen	78
	Sam Small leaves town	Manning	78
	Our Island Nation		
1939	Co-Operette		79
1941	Major Barbara	prologue	94
1942	Salute John Citizen	Oskey	94
1944	This Happy Breed	Bob Mitchell	97

'Alive and Kicking'.

Stanley Holloway with Robertson Hare - *One Wild Oat*

Appendix 'C'

Stage Shows in which Stanley Holloway appeared.

Title	Theatre	Date
Kissing Time	Winter Gdns, Drury Lane	1919
A night out	- ditto -	1920
Hit the Deck	London Hippodrome	1927
A song of the sea	His Majesty's	1928
Here we are again	Lyceum	1932
The three sisters	Drury Lane	1934
Life begins at Oxford Circus	London Palladium	1935
All Wave	Duke of York's	1936
London Rhapsody	Palladium	1938
Up and doing	Saville	1940
Fine and Dandy	Saville	1942
A Midsummer Night's dream	Edinburgh Metropolitan Opera, New York	1954 1954
My Fair Lady	Mark Hellinger	1956
My Fair Lady	Drury Lane	1958
Candida	Niagara, Shaw Festival, Canada	1970
Siege	Cambridge	1972
You never can tell	Shaw festival Canada	1973

Appendix 'D'

Pantomimes in which Stanley Holloway performed.

Name	Place	Date
Aladdin	Prince of Wales, Birmingham	1934
"	Leeds	1935
"	Golders Green Hippodrome	1936
"	Edinburgh	1937
"	Manchester	1938
Mother Goose	London Casino	1946
Aladdin	South Africa tour	1951
Peter Pan		1953

Humorous poetry	Recorded in 1960
How pleasant to know Mr. Lear	by Edward Lear

The ape and the lady	)	These Bab ballads of
The yarn of the 'Nancy Bell	)	
Peter the wag,	)	W.S. Gilbert were
The sensation captain	)	
Ben Allah Achmet or the Fatal Tum	)	recorded on Caedmon
Phrenology,	)	
Babettes Love.	)	TC 1104

Joyce Grenfell on reverse.

A star never to be forgotten

Gorleston,
The Gazette 18 May 1990

NEXT week on the Britannia Pier Yarmouth Amateur Operatic and Dramatic Society is staging the popular musical "My Fair Lady."

Julia Canwell as Eliza and Michael Rodgers as her father Alfred Doolittle have to contend with the intelligent gamble of Michael Mills as Professor Higgins and his aide Terry Bird as Colonel Pickering.

The famous music directed by John Roper and the whole produced by Jack Bacon offer fine family entertainment, from May 26 to June 2.

For 30 years since the Drury Lane production audiences have loved this Shavian, rags to riches version of "Pygmalion."

Amateur societies up and down the country have been glad to keep this show alive and two other versions have pleased at Fakenham and Hunstanton recently.

The leading parts don't have to compete with Rex Harrison, Julie Andrews/Audrey Hepburn and Stanley Holloway, although the 1964 film is re-shown on television and available on video.

Chat

One of the original cast for the Broadway 1956 production very nearly walked out!

Moss Hart the producer had not called him to rehearsal which tried his patience and seemed insulting.

At a famous chat it was apparently said: "Look Mr. Holloway, I've got to teach Rex Harrison to sing, Julie Andrews to be a coarse Cockney, but I know you can sing and dance through what I want straightaway."

So fortunately Stanley Holloway stayed and deserved his nomination for an Oscar.

Who would have thought from October 1, 1890 at Manor Park, London E12, 100 years ago, such a varied stage career would stem, ending at the top of his profession with an OBE?

From popular choirboy, before radio and TV could have equalled Aled Jones, he performed in the local church. He was asked to sing at clubs before going off to France in 1914.

On return he teamed up with Leslie Henson in the Co-optimists.

Their successful pierrot seaside entertainment programme was the first to appear in London's West End at the Royalty Theatre in 1921.

In 1928 the introduction of the monologue secured his place in British hearts and memories.

Sam Small and his musket with the Duke of Wellington was always enjoyed.

Today, Ian Wallace recalls his eighth birthday treat at Golders Green Hippodrome was hearing it and birthday wishes from the stage by the great character.

Heyday

Albert and the Lion followed and many thought Stanley Holloway a north countryman not a Cockney. Gracie Fields in her heyday suggested Holloway had enough good material and style to do shows on his own. Radio was founded at Savoy Hill and his voice was heard.

The British Film industry was developing and he made a mark in "Sing As We Go."

Later in "The Perfect Woman," "Titfield Thunderbolt," "Passport to Pimlico" and "The Lavender Hill Mob," Stanley Holloway secured his place with cinema-going audiences.

Shakespeare, too, has a place for amusing characters and Hamlet's gravedigger for Alec Guiness and then Laurence Olivier and as Bottom, in "A Midsummer Night's Dream" with Moira Shearer, exercised Holloway's talents well.

Sir Alec Guiness still remembers their collaboration and writes: "He was a delightful, cheerful and kind man." Sir Alec also recalls a surprise birthday party at the Savoy Hotel organised a bit like "This Is Your Life."

In New York while appearing in Shakespeare, two men named Lerner and Loewe saw the man they needed for Alfred Doolittle for their new production.

We know now how wise their choice was. In 1959 an Order of the British Empire and Variety Club of Great Britain Special Award in 1973 achknowledged his skilful wide range of roles.

In January, 1982 the Times newspaper outlined the 92 years of the "Rumbustious Cockney Entertainer" while his local paper in Sussex talked of "Stanley - Doolittle who did so much."

As a cricket fan he had mildly hoped to "make a tun perhaps". Wiv a little bit of luck his life and work won't be forgotten. Did your grandma or grandpa see him at Catlin's Mitchell Craig Sunday night shows at the Wellington Pavilion?

Roy Walding

SAM'S FORTUNE.

It happened one evening in Wigan at a certain men's club I could name

We were some of us standing round talking and some of us playing a game

When all of a sudden Fred Higgins came hurrying into the place

and something unusual had happened we saw from the look on his face.

I've just heard the news, gasped Fred Higgins knocking back the first drink that he found

Sam's uncle has left him a fortune one hundred and fifty odd pounds.

Then in through that door at that moment there stepped the spoilt darling of fate

walked the hero himself of our story - Sam the heir to his uncle's estate.

And just as though nothing had happened Sam walks up as cool as can be

Good evening he says to young Lily I'll have a good strong cuppa tea

Ee lad returned Lily in fun like you never came up here on tram

youv'e got money to ride in a taxi nay I'm going to invest it says Sam.

Before Sam has finished his stirring Mr. Murgatroyd draws him aside

I've a great proposition he whispers a greyhound her names Blushing Bride ,

A fellow I know knows a fella whose brothers a pal of two chaps

who reckons her owner would sell her for a hundred and fifty perhaps ,

Imagine you owning a greyhound and cutting an elegant dash

champagne and cigars for the asking while your greyhound is earning you cash

you can't help but make a big fortune though you don't know a dog from a lamb

replacing his cup in his saucer I'm going to invest it says Sam

not half an hour later Fred Higgins comes up as Sam looks down his cue

Ee Sam I've just had a brainwave, I'm passing it straight on to you the way to big money is pictures imagine the studio life

you sit in a chair by the camera and send messages home to your wife.

Don't wait up for me you informer I'm working till late on the floor

I may not get home til tomorrow if the picture's not finished before.

and when a young man plays a love scene you show him just what should be done

and pick pretty girls for the crowd scenes, having taken good look at each one.

So you know where you are while its rolling I tell you it's money for jam

but Sam shook his head as he went in off red I'm going to invest it said Sam.

Old Briggs was the next to approach him he went up to Sam playing darts

have you ever, said Joe, thought of cruising around the south seas and them parts

you sit on the deck in your yacht cap while waiters fly round with a whizz

and Lady Fitznoodle comes by with her poodle and says what a fine day it is

she tells you about her rheumatics you tell of yours once or twice

and the duke he comes out with a tale of his gout and it's all very homely and nice.

Aye all things considered I think you should travel to Southport, Southend or Siam

as he finished his score with a neat double four nay I'm going to invest it says Sam

then Lily chipped in with a notion take a tip Sam from one of the girls

opportunity this is to dress up the missus and buy her a small string of pearls

or get something cheaper a new carpet sweeper, piano or radiogram .

Nay Lily says he as he paid for his tea I'm going to invest it says Sam

now just at that moment a stranger came hurrying into the hall

he looks round on the assemble which gent he enquired is Sam Small?

"I am" answered Sam "have you got it? Rather" said the stranger "don't fear when I called at the house your good lady requested I bring her up here".

Outside queried Sam and we followed he hurried out into the street

leaving Murgatroyd Sterling and Higgins in amazement profound and complete

that hundred and fifty you told us "I'm going to invest it I am".

So I am he replied in an Austin and I'm proud of me judgement says Sam

goes faster than yon blushing greyhound looks better than filmstars on set

and as for the pleasure of travel its equal I've not seen as yet ₜ

'Twas one of them Austin big sevens that do sixty on top and no buts

developing 25 horse power not only got looks but got guts

it does forty miles to the gallon got plenty of room and good lines

if they gong us between here and Blackpool says Sam I've got ten bob left over for fines.

(The Commercial was made with Stanley Holloway for the Austin Motor Company,
Longbridge Birmingham)

Stanley Holloway was a very versatile performer, from 1915 to 1975.

Roy Walding was educated at Luton Grammar School, Beds. After service in the Royal Air Force in Southern Rhodesia, he went to St. Paul's College Cheltenham and the City of Sheffield Teacher Training College. He took early retirement in 1986 from primary Headship

In 1987, Mr. Walding began to research the life of Stanley Holloway, whom he had seen performing at Drury Lane in 1959. Local B.B.C. Radio Norfolk were interested in the work. A programme about of Stanley Holloway celebrating the centenary of his birth was broadcast on B.B.C. Radio 2 in 1990, called - 'Pull out the stopper' presented by Ian Wallace.

Mr Walding added other subjects to the illustrated talks offered to various groups. The History of the Music Hall, 1860-1910, Lives of Gilbert and Sullivan, Gracie Fields, Noel Coward and Joyce Grenfell were all researched and have been well received. Such activity in his Third Age has been rewarding. Older readers and younger students of Traditional Art Forms, enjoy remembering or finding out more about our entertainers.

"Well it was fun while it lasted" were words spoken by Stanley Holloway (as the benevolent Mr. Valentine) in the film *Titfield Thunderbolt* The words seem to sum up his career ranging from choirboy, to soldier, Concert party pierrot, Co-Optimist, stage and film actor,(including Shakespearean experience). He reached the pinnacle of his career as Alfred Doolittle in *My Fair Lady* seen on stage and screen, when he was well over 60.

Mr. Walding, with the help of his friend in Birmingham has found much more information confirming how really talented and versatile Stanley Holloway really was. Putting together the pieces of the jigsaw of his life in this book, has been fascinating retirement activity

Roy Walding, October,1996

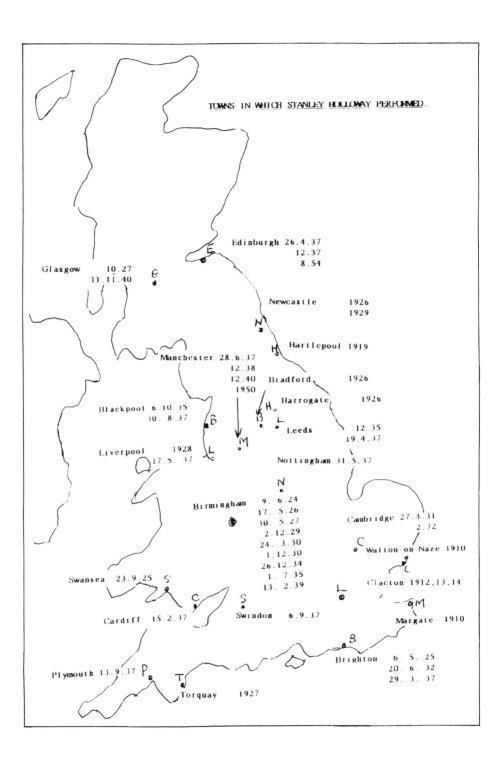

TOWNS IN WHICH STANLEY HOLLOWAY PERFORMED.

Edinburgh 26.4.37
12.37
8.54

Glasgow 10.27
11.11.40

Newcastle 1926
1929

Hartlepool 1919

Manchester 28.6.37
12.38
12.40
1950

Bradford 1926

Harrogate 1926

Blackpool 6.10.35
30.8.37

Leeds 12.35
19.4.37

Liverpool 1928
17.5.37

Nottingham 31.5.37

Birmingham 9.6.24
17.5.26
30.5.27
2.12.29
24.3.30
1.12.30
26.12.34
1.7.35
13.2.39

Cambridge 27.4.31
2.72

Walton-on-Naze 1910

Clacton 1912,13,14

Swansea 23.9.25

Cardiff 15.2.37

Swindon 6.9.37

Margate 1910

Brighton 6.5.25
20.6.32
29.3.37

Plymouth 13.9.37

Torquay 1927

NEW THEATRE
CAMBRIDGE
700.

TELEPHONE _____

Six Nights at 8.15.

MONDAY, APRIL 27th, 1931.   Matinee, Saturday at 2.30.

The Original
CO - OPTIMISTS
Themselves

Written by GREATREX NEWMAN. Music by BILLY MAYERL. Additional Lyrics by FRANK EYTON.
Dances by FRED LORD. Produced by LADDIE CLIFF. Orchestra under the direction of S. J. GROVE.

PART I.

1.—THE CO-OPTIMISTS re-introduce themselves with their accustomed modesty. " Cheero Pierrot."

2.—DAVY BURNABY (Greater than Ever). " The Old Guard." Supported by entire Star Company, including Martell and Hennessey.

3.—STANLEY HOLLOWAY will sing about " The King who wanted Jam for Tea."

4.—BETTY CHESTER, being " The Bandmaster's Daughter " will endeavour to beat the Band.

5.—BILLY MAYERL in a spectacular presentation of Oriental Splendour " My Turkish Delight " (proving that the Yeast rises even higher than the vest).

6.—SYLVIA CECIL will point " The Road to Fairyland " (A.A. Loop Way).

7.—PHYLLIS MONKMAN and TEDDY FOX take steps to entertain. " Maybe it's You."

8.—MARRIOTT EDGAR strikes out. " The Channel Swimmer."

9.—THE CO-OPTIMISTS' rendition of " Jack and Jill." A pail phantom of the well-known nursery rhyme.

PART II.

1.—TEDDY FOX trailed by Total Tribe of Terpsichorean Tartars will urge you to " Dance Your Troubles Away."

2.—CO-OPTIMISTS' PUNISHMENT entitled " Spring Punions."

3.—PEGGY PETRONELLA will Dance for you.

4.—SYLVIA CECIL will sing " One Morning Very Early " (by permission of the Milkmen's Union).

5.—THE LEARNINGHAM REPERTORY CO. present ALL their " Detachable Dramas."

6.—PHYLLIS MONKMAN and BILLY MAYERL take a flight of fancy, " Sky Lady."

7.—" GREAT STUFF THIS EDUCATION "—A Harrowing episode—

Mr. Butterworth	DAVY BURNABY
Mr. Entwhistle	STANLEY HOLLOWAY
Master John Entwhistle	BOBBY ALDERSON

8.—BETTY CHESTER sings " What wouldn't I do for that Man."

9.—" THE LOST CHILD " The effect of the Russian Ballet

The Nursemaid	PEGGY PETRONELLA
Doctor Dear	TEDDY FOX
Policeman...	DAVY BURNABY
Man-about-Town	MARRIOTT EDGAR

10.—STANLEY HOLLOWAY. A voice and some mimicry.

11.—PHYLLIS MONKMAN and MARRIOTT EDGAR. " The Clean Up " (Direct from the Ziegfeld Follies). (Parisian creation worn in this scene executed by Nanti Metza et Cie).

12.—TWO PIANOS—Oh yes, and BILLY MAYERL.

13.—DAVY BURNABY and entire Band of Hope and Glory. " Schultz is Back Again." Introducing the famous Co-Optimists' String Band (which when travelling is used for tying up the bags).

THE
·1935·
ROYAL VARIETY
PERFORMANCE

29 October
London Palladium
In the presence of Their Majesties King George V and Queen Mary
Presented by George Black
Musical Director – Richard Crean

THE PROGRAMME

Hannah Watt, Jeanne Devereaux, Nervo and Knox, Naughton and Gold, Flanagan and Allen, Ernie
Gerrard, the Six Lias in 'A Flower Market' from *Round About Regent Street*
The Diamond Brothers – Acrobatic Dancing Comedians
Joe Jackson – 'Silent Comedy'
Stanley Holloway – Monologues
Anton Dolin, Jessie Matthews, J. Sherman Fisher's Palladium Girls in 'A Feathered Flirtation'
The Western Brothers – Entertainers
'Old London Town', excerpts from *Round About Regent Street* with Jeanne Devereaux, Hannah Watt,
Harrison and Fisher, Myles Williams, Flanagan and Allen, The Harmony Revellers, Bea Hutten, Syd
Railton, Del Foss, Nervo and Knox, Naughton and Gold
Boy Foy – England's Youngest Juggler
Sandy Powell with Jimmy Fletcher and Roy Jeffries in 'The Test Match'
Three Cossacks – Roller Skaters
Elsie Carlisle & Sam Browne – Radio Entertainers
Will Mahoney – American Comedian
Arthur Reece, Kate Carney, Gus Elen, Florrie Forde, Harry Champion in 'Cavalcade of Variety',
introduced by Stanley Holloway
Harry Roy & His Band

For Roy
in gratitude for
great help on
The Stanley Holloway
Centenary programme

8th August - 1990

**IAN
WALLACE**

ALEC GUINNESS

Comedy Theatre
Pantou St.
London, W.1.

6.2.89

Dear Mr. Walding

Thank you for your kind letter.

Stanley Holloway was a delightful, cheerful and kind man. I only worked with him once — Lavender Hill Mob. The best person to contact would be his son, but I fear I have no address. British Actors Equity, 8 Harley Street, W.1. would probably find him. The last time I saw him was at a private lunch, for about 20,

given on his 70° (?) birthday. Stanley didn't know it was on — he thought he was just lunching alone with his son. We happened to go into The Savoy together and he kept spotting old friends (the lunch had been kept a secret) and greeting them with, "Fancy seeing you here!" Not until we got into the dining room did the penny drop that it was a lunch in his honour. He was knocked sideways by it but very delighted.

Yours sincerely,
Alec Guinness

The British Broadcasting Corporation

Head Office: Broadcasting House, London W1A 1AA Tel. 01-580 4468

XXXXXXXXXXXXXXXXXXXXXXXXXXXXXXXXXX
XXXXXXXXXXXXXXXX Telephone: XXXXXXXXXXXXXXXXXXX

071-927

A/C use only

Talks Requisi
1. Contributor (
2. Contributor t
   and Return
3. Registry

BBC Reference: XX/ 03/RAC/KM Ext: 4722 Date: 20.07.90

Offer of engagement to you for the contribution(s) described below at the fee specified in the form of acceptance and on the terms and conditions set out on this page and overleaf relating to all types of contributions and to contributions.

TALKS
Prog. No.

ROY WALDING

90ZA7080GLO.

Service	
Title:	Radio 4.
	Paypoint: LONDON.

Duration/nature of contribution:
(Note: Final manuscripts of scripted talks contributions must be received by the BBC not later than ten days before the broadcast or recording date(s) unless otherwise agreed.)

"STANLEY HOLLOWAY" (W/T)

REcord interview with Ian Wallace for Holloway documentary (3.mins.max).

Rehearsal/Recording date(s) and time(s):

8th August 1990.

Location/Studio

LONDON.

Transmission date(s) and time(s):

2nd October 1990.
21.02.

Producer's name
(and signature if appropriate)
Fee:

Nick Clarke EXT:

Date:

£50.00 (SPECIAL) + £41.00 r/f

If you wish to accept please sign the form of acceptance in Part B below of copy No. 2. This offer may be cancelled if your si
not received within ten days of this offer. If the fee proposed below is paid before we receive your signed acceptance of this c
shall be at liberty to treat your acceptance of the payment as confirmation that you accept the contract. If you receive notice
defamation in respect of your contribution(s), you are asked to notify the BBC before taking any steps to deal with the claim.

Signed on behalf of the BBC

For signature by the contributor. I accept the offer in consideration of the fee mentioned above and on the terms and (

Date: 24-7-90 .... Contributor's signature: ....

KEN McHALE

SIGNED ACCEPTANCE COPY No. 2 TO BE RETURNE
SIGNATORY AT ADDRESS ABOVE